What Does God Want Me to Do?

Clem Boyd

What Does God Want Me to Do?

Learn from Others
the Right Road for You

TATE PUBLISHING & *Enterprises*

Published by Tate Publishing & Enterprises, LLC
127 E. Trade Center Terrace | Mustang, Oklahoma 73064 USA
1.888.361.9473 | www.tatepublishing.com

Tate Publishing is committed to excellence in the publishing industry. The company reflects the philosophy established by the founders, based on Psalm 68:11,
"The Lord gave the word and great was the company of those who published it."

Book design copyright © 2008 by Tate Publishing, LLC. All rights reserved.
Cover design by Stephanie Woloszyn
Interior design by Summer Floyd-Harvey

Published in the United States of America

ISBN: 978-1-60604-882-5
1. Motivational Christian Living
2. Personal Growth, Relationships
08.12.05

To Julia, David, Bethany, and Mark, who help me every day to follow God's leading in my life.

To my parents, Clem and Jean Boyd, who gave me the love and encouragement to explore my God-given design.

Acknowledgments

Thank you, Kathy (Heine) Cheek and Dee (Rausch) Junkins. These two women explained the Gospel to me and answered my questions when I was a senior in college. Without them I may never have met Jesus and this book would never have been written. You were brave, patient, and kind.

Through my wife, Julia, and three children, David, Bethany, and Mark, God has introduced me to a whole way of life beyond my dreams as a young man. I could not imagine life without them now. Thanks for bringing so much of God's love and joy into my life.

My sincere gratitude goes to the following people who read this manuscript and offered input and encouragement: Julia Boyd, Roger Brucker, Betty Carano, Andrea Jewell, Gary DeLashmutt, Dave Howard, Phil Wong, Monte Wolverton, Dean Ridings, Tom Hess, and Rob Dant.

Thanks also to the many people who allowed me to use their stories in this book, all of which made *What Does God Want Me to Do?* more complete.

Table of Contents

Introduction

This used to be a completely different book. It was an autobiographical story about the lessons God had taught me on my way to being a caregiver dad and freelance writer. My wife observed that it wasn't really about that, but it was about making sacrifices for the greater good of God and family.

Till then I had been struggling with the book. But Julia's comments clarified the reason why: I didn't see any particular glory in being a caregiver dad. I love what I do, but it's not for all men, or women. Rather, it's one example of a believer in God trying to obey the creator's leading in his life.

My response to God resulted in the life I'm living today as a father and husband, church leader, freelance magazine journalist, and author. As I continue to follow his direction, my life circumstances will change. I could work full time at a magazine or publishing company because of his promptings. Perhaps I'll work as a teacher. Maybe Julia and I will end up on the mission field. I don't know; God does, and that's fine. The content of our life should be written by him.

When I viewed the book through the lens of making life alterations for the sake of following God's call, I saw this project from a larger perspective. The wheels unlocked, the pistons began to fire, and my brain started to rev up. I began to think of people who had made some kind of change in their lives because they were trying to obey the Holy Spirit's nudging and prodding. I was getting jazzed, pumped up, enthused—choose your adjective—about the work. Either that or the caffeine had finally kicked in.

As wonderful as my life is to me, the more wonderful thing is seeing any person abandon themselves to a God who's worth the risk. And this is why you presently sit, stand, or recline with this book in hand. I hope you will uncover in these pages ideas that steer you toward the life God had in mind for you when he wove your DNA strand. May you experience an overabundance of his blessings as you begin your own great adventure.

Section 1: Imagine a Different Life

You've been on a certain life path for some time now. What if there's more? What if God intends something different for you, for your family, for your future?

The chapters in this section ask a series of questions:

- Why am I thinking about this?
- Who am I anyway?
- What will it cost?
- How will I get there?

As you contemplate the answer to each question, I pray it clarifies the nature of this divine quest and the reason you're making it. Happy exploring!

Why Am I Thinking about This?

Here's a story: there was a guy who worked sixty to seventy hours a week, rarely saw his family, was a loving father and husband when he was around, and attended church regularly when he wasn't on a business trip. He retired in his sixties, and died a year or so afterwards. The end.

For many that's the story of their lives. Unless, of course, you're reading these pages, which means you're not dead. And that's good. Because while you're still alive there's still the potential for change, if change is what you seek.

American life is about living large and going fast and pushing forward. How many societies get as pumped up about something so bland as "worker productivity"? Yet newspapers around the country will excitedly announce surges in productivity as a sign of a robust economy. Or, conversely, that things are going bad because productivity is in the toilet.

How many societies fixate on how many extra-curricular activities their kids are doing? Or agonize over the quality of those after-school commitments? And what that will mean for their future?

Many people faithfully carry out their roles as defined by society or family expectations. Even though there may be plenty of relentless pushing and moving, they get into comfortable grooves. These grooves may not be exactly satisfying or enriching, but they have the approval of others and come with a sense that "at least I'm doing something."

These life niches come with something else that's quite important—predictability. Grinding, unstopping predictability. Sure, there's the occasional hiccup in the schedule, and Joe and Susan may feel rushed now and then; but they have a certain amount of certainty. And they like that. I like predictability too.

I always wanted to be a writer. In fourth grade my best friend and I published a homeroom newspaper using the school mimeograph machine: *The 104 News.* Great title: straightforward, to the point. I still have a copy somewhere.

While I looked into different careers in high school and college, my path didn't veer far from writing or communications. I attended Ohio University in Athens, Ohio, a school known for its excellent journalism program.

After college I held several writing jobs before settling as a newspaper reporter. I worked for a chain of community newspapers for several years then transitioned to a job as beat reporter with a small daily near my hometown. Things were moving along briskly. I could see my journalism career going somewhere. And then I swerved off the career path.

The choices I made in life, since those days of working as a beat writer in Xenia, Ohio, are not choices I can recommend to everyone. They're choices that spring from who I am and the interests and values I share with my wife, Julia, a part-time family practice doctor.

I work part time as a church leader and freelance writer out of a home-based office, taking care of my kids four half days a week. I keep a schedule that allows me to respond to spur of the moment opportunities to do things I think God wants me to do with family and friends.

Not everyone wants what I have, and what I have isn't for everyone. But this isn't about becoming a stay-at-home dad or a telecommuter. This is about looking at life and figuring out if God's priorities direct the action.

• • • •

Life-Changing Discussion

• • • •

Back when Julia and I were talking about marriage, we talked frankly about the direction of our lives. At the time I was a newspaper editor and Julia was in her third year of residency as a family practice doctor, just a couple months from going into practice.

We talked mainly about kids and childcare, but the conversation evolved into something else: being there for parents, making friendships with brothers and sisters in Christ, and the kind of atmosphere we wanted in our home. Looking back I realize we were having a discussion about values: what were Julia's values and what were mine.

Values drive decision-making. Making lots of money and having the nicest house is a value with a capital "V." Important decisions affecting every other area of life will flow from that. Wanting plenty of free time to support political or social causes is a value, so is raising kids to attend church or not attend church, to play sports or not play sports, visit art museums, go on vacations, or root for a favorite team.

Many people don't think about their values, out loud at least. Their values remain secluded in the shady portions of their minds, concealed but barking orders like a marine drill sergeant—"you will drive the nice car; you will work eighty hours a week; you will have three beautiful children"—and on and on.

Where do values come from? The answer is simple: everywhere—television, movies, newspapers, magazines, books, peers. Parents have a major impact on values, whether to model mom and dad's priorities or react against them.

Other significant adults often shape values. It may be a sibling, an uncle or aunt, a soccer or football coach, a favorite teacher. It may be something they said, choices they made, or the life they lived that left an impression.

Then there's the all-pervasive media. Does Madison Avenue really shape values? Well, it sure tries to, and not just passively, but with vigor. The billions of dollars spent on advertising each year testifies to that. I hope there's not much doubt about that in this give-me-more consumer society.

But what about the Bible? Christians' values *should*

be changing and rearranging according to what God's truth says. This is what Paul means in Romans 12:

> Do not conform any longer to the pattern of this world, but be *transformed by the renewing of your mind.* Then you will be able to test and approve what God's will is—his good, pleasing and perfect will.
>
> (Romans 12:2, NIV; emphasis added)

According to 2 Timothy 3:16–17, God breathed the words of Scripture into existence, just as he spoke the world into existence. These words are useful for "teaching, correcting, rebuking and training in righteousness so that the man of God may be thoroughly equipped for every good work" (NIV).

To live a life of "good works" will require a transformation of my mind. I will need to saturate myself in the truths of God; I must allow the Bible to teach me, correct me, rebuke me, and train me about what it means to live a righteous life. I should listen as Christian friends and spiritual mentors challenge me and encourage me with scriptural truth. Then I will have values that more and more reflect God's values, resulting in a life of eternal significance.

And here's the top value I should embrace above all others: my ultimate worth comes from the fact that God loves me and has saved me from his judgment. From God's point of view, the biggest thing that ever happened in my life was the day I asked his Son to be my savior. At that point, I went from eternal separation from God to union with him, from war to peace, from judgment to forgiveness, from insignificance to significance, from unacceptable to accepted for all time, from creature made in God's image to his child.

Julia and I wouldn't even have had the what-about-kids discussion and its related subtopics unless we had begun the transformation described above. There was a significant conclusion from our discussion: the way we defined ourselves would have to rest more securely in what God said, rather than what our jobs said or significant people said. Seeing career as a variable rather than a given was the result.

There were implications for the way we viewed our stuff too. Our home, instead of a private retreat, would be a foyer for God's kingdom. Strangers would always be welcome. Our kids would get introduced to all kinds of people and develop important friendships with adults other than family members. We would have to teach them that a house is a gift from God to be used at his discretion, even though we were the ones who lived there most of the time. Our things might get broken, scuffed up or lost. But it would all be worth it.

• • • •

The Bigger Question

• • • •

All this talk about rearranging and reshuffling is dependent on the answer to a bigger question: have you been changed on the inside?

I'm not talking about going to church, singing hymns, putting money in the plate, or attending Sunday school. Have I ever asked God to forgive me because of his Son's sacrifice for my sins? That's the pivotal question. This might turn off some folks; they've heard the wacko Christians go on about this. Please don't close the book and walk away. Indulge me for a few more minutes.

Consider the example of Cornelius. Cornelius was

an extremely religious guy. He gave scads of money to the poor and talked to God regularly. Yet this man was missing something. So God sent Peter to explain who Jesus was and what Jesus did. Then Cornelius believed in Jesus and accepted his death as satisfaction of the moral debt he owed God. The whole story is delivered in greater detail in the New Testament book of Acts, chapter ten.

Had I been alive at that time, I might have assumed that Cornelius was a Christian. But he wasn't. Something was missing in the spiritual wiring, which hearing and believing the story of Jesus resolved. Once Cornelius believed in Jesus as his savior, he received the Holy Spirit. And according to Romans 8:9, if I don't have the Holy Spirit in my soul, I still don't belong to God, no matter how much good I do or how nice I am.

In his story about the life of Jesus, the apostle John notes that people need to actually invite Christ, who is still alive, into their lives. He writes:

> Yet to all who received him, to those who believed in his name, he gave the right to become children of God—children born not of natural descent, nor of human decision or a husband's will, but born of God.
>
> JOHN 1:12–13 (NIV)

How do I make the invitation? I might talk to God like this:

"Lord, forgive me for my wrong thoughts and wrong actions. I know I deserve hell, but I believe your Son wiped out my guilt for all time, clearing me of the evil I've done or imagined in the past, present, and future. I ask him right now to come into my life and show me how to follow you."

Praying that prayer will start a relationship with God that has nothing to do with how good you are or how often you attend church. This will change the eternal outcome of your life immediately. Plus, having the Holy Spirit on board will be a great help with a book like this, so you can capture and apply the most from it (see John 14:26 and John 16:13).

• • • •

The Need for Change

• • • •

Combinations of events and realizations spur change. It could be the birth of a child or the death of a parent or both. Maybe a person is fired or laid off or didn't get the promotion she thought she was getting. Or she did get the promotion and the raise, but life got harder instead of better. Perhaps the kids are getting ready to leave the nest. Everyone gets wake-up calls; the real question is whether they jump out of their beds of complacency or hit the mental snooze button.

At age twenty-seven, I could not have imagined making some of the choices I've ended up making. My macho focus wouldn't allow the idea of not being the big provider. Here are a few of the "ah-ha" moments and circumstances that God used to change my worldly perspective so that I might adopt his point of view:

Income disparity - One thing was very clear at the beginning of our marriage—Julia could work part-time and still make more money than I could make full-time. If raising kids and being available for ministry were our values then we'd have to bank our money and time wisely. I began to see this would affect me.

Our kids - My son David was born in 1992. Holding him and spending time with him awakened my daddy instinct in a way that would change my life. This only heightened with the births of Bethany and Mark. I wanted to have a greater role in the lives of my children, and not just after working eight to twelve hours a day for the newspaper.

The Holy Spirit has strongly impressed me that one of my greatest Great Commission legacies (see Matthew 28:18–20) will be my children. Would I give the Lord the carte blanche to use me, along with Julia, to shape them into people who knew Jesus, loved Jesus, and wanted to give their lives to others as he had? I have come to the conclusion that, even if I were to win a Pulitzer but not be a *major* player in God's game plan for my children, I would be a failure.

Plus, I must admit, I have fun with my kids. I totally enjoyed helping David build Lego villages when he was three, which he would play with for a while, then destroy like Godzilla in Tokyo. I loved pretending to be pirates on our gym set. I got a kick out of speaking for my daughter's Ken doll and inserting life philosophy in his comments to Barbie, "Really Barbie, I like your pink convertible, but I think getting married on the first date is a little sudden. But you do look cute in your princess dress." I'm refreshed in a deep way when I take walks with Mark in the woods near our house and we happen to see a deer cross our path. Awesome isn't a big enough word for what these times mean to me.

Going back to school - In 1993 my love of building relationships with people for God's purposes won out over writing about car crashes and school levy campaigns. I could work as a journalist and follow God. Who knows, I may end up covering a beat again someday. But making God-centered relationships a priority means that other things become less of a priority, and that's how it went in 1993 with newspaper deadlines. I decided to pursue further education at a seminary in Cincinnati, which I hoped would prepare me for more effective people involvement. However, it also required saying goodbye to the journalism career ladder for the time.

Lois' death - After seminary I began spending more time watching the kids, with my mother-in-law, Lois Sammons, covering the times I worked part time as a media relations coordinator and fundraiser for a local hospice program. But then Lois' breast cancer, in remission five years, metastasized to her brain. She went into the hospice program I worked for and died just before Easter 1997.

I had always imagined going back to work full-time, although I was hoping I could do that through our church. I had never seen myself *not* doing that. But something changed after Lois died. Maybe I became adjusted to the idea of taking on more of the caregiver role. Maybe I had worked through some key things about the way I saw myself. My sense of self-worth was coming less and less from having a successful career, as the world defined it. More and more I was being fulfilled through ministry, family life, and the work God had given me.

Satisfied by freelancing - After seminary I submitted story proposals to Christian magazines and eventually got my first sale with *Plain Truth Magazine* in 1997. By 1998 I was beginning to make headway with freelancing: I had a formal contract to produce a news insert for Focus on the Family's *Citizen* magazine and landing a variety of assignments from other publications.

For me, the adventure of researching a story has always been satisfying. I love the mental piston-firing experience involved in producing a written work. E-mailing the polished article to an editor on time, especially with a tough topic on a tight deadline, produces a unique strain of adrenaline-packed contentment. Who needs a title when you've already got the greatest job in the world? I can think about and investigate a topic and then get paid for my research and observations. How great is that?

The availability dividend - Being available has its own upside, which is very appealing. Because of my schedule, I'm flexible to meet other guys for lunch or breakfast and talk about their lives, my life, what God is showing us, how the favorite sports team is doing, etc. This can mean that I'm actually busier at times than I would be with an eight-to-five job, but I've concluded that's how God wants my life to be. And there's tremendous satisfaction I experience because of my elastic schedule.

• • • •

The Context of Significance

• • • •

Most of the New Testament's message about God's plan is in the context of fulfilling a role I've been given in his worldwide endeavor called the church. The role I have to play is primarily local, carrying out numerous kinds of service with other people, especially in small communities of Christians where I learn how to love others as Jesus Christ has loved me. This is God's main means for getting the word out about his Son to those who don't know him (John 13:34).

God's view of significance is through the lens of relationships—who I'm supposed to connect with and the way I'm letting him use me to benefit others and vice versa. These relationships naturally include my spouse and children.

How many hours does the average person clock at his job: forty, fifty, sixty hours, or more? Even if my work hours are fairly reasonable, how much am I really "there" when I see my wife, my kids, or friends?

Maybe you're the caregiver parent and see yourself primarily in that role. This is good; there should be more parents devoted to this job. But perhaps you're beginning to wonder if God wants to expand your horizons, get you out of the house a little bit during the day because he wants you to disciple, evangelize, and otherwise care about others. This may mean taking the kids out of the house while you have lunch with some friends, or calling on a friend to watch the children occasionally while you volunteer at a homeless shelter or lead a teen Bible study. We need to ask ourselves a question at this point: Is my view of myself in Christ strong enough to permit flexibility in the amount of time I spend parenting?

Perhaps you're retired. You've done your bit for the economy and you're ready for some rest and leisure. *I've been putting off that model railroading hobby for years, and now it's time to get serious*, you think to yourself. *I've always wanted to learn how to take amazing photographs but never had the time*. Is that the end of it? We could be on the threshold of the most significant period in our lives. We ought to ask: what does the Lord want me to do?

Students may look at their near futures as pretty much laid out for them: attend high school and finish in four years, attend a trade or technical school for two years, or go to college for four to six years, maybe pursue a graduate degree. Someone else tells you the requirements, and you just fill in the schedule blanks like a Sudoku puzzle. You have a few extra-curricular activities you enjoy. But have you ever pulled back and evaluated, from a prayerful, God-centered angle with the help of prayerful, God-centered people why you're doing what you're doing?

In addition to ministry and service, God's plan is also moral. He wants to see character change, which has implications for my relationships and the effect I have on others. He wants to see the fruit of a life led more and more by His Spirit—love, joy, peace, patience, kindness, goodness, faithfulness, gentleness, and self-control (Galatians 5:22–23). He wants to see my choices about career and family and everything else have more and more his moral stamp. This is something he's committed to accomplishing in me, if I'm willing to cooperate.

Some may think, "Doing more for God sounds great—where do I sign up and not upset my current lifestyle too much?"

I've spent years trying to figure that out. I like my comfort as much as anyone, and yet I also want to make a difference for God that will change the substance of eternity. The quality and content of forever, mine and I hope many others, hinges on the choices I make about the small and large parts of my ordinary, everyday reality. What will I choose?

This dilemma is similar to the one Jesus spelled out:

> No one can serve two masters. Either he will hate the one and love the other, or he will be devoted to the one and despise the other.
>
> MATTHEW 6:24 (NIV)

In context, Jesus was describing the impossibility of devotion to God and devotion to material comfort. These are mutually exclusive.

Being more available for God's purposes may mean taking a job with less pay. Or it might mean interrupting the flow of your current day-to-day schedule with the kids. Or it could mean surrendering that beloved retirement hobby to his timing and plan. Or looking into a course of study that your parents may or may not understand or even appreciate. Following God means taking chances; there's no getting around the risks.

Here's something else to consider: in American society, if co-workers think someone's not giving 120 percent to the job it can result in a loss of prestige. Jeff Gordon, a Columbus, Ohio, internist, faced exactly this. There were fellow doctors who questioned his "commitment" to medicine because of his choice to be more available for ministry in his church and to his wife and children.

Did Jeff's job choice suddenly make him less competent? Did he suffer an abrupt loss of medical expertise? No, of course he didn't. But he was willing to risk the estimation of others to pursue a bigger purpose.

There are potential costs of making such a decision that must be tallied. If those costs aren't considered, you might make choices which lead to frustration later. I didn't understand all of those costs myself and experienced resentment and discouragement that I hope others do not experience.

I remember getting quite agitated one afternoon during graduate school when my oldest son was a toddler. *I should be out there tracking down criminals, interviewing cops and detectives, and beating a deadline, not making macaroni and cheese,* was how it went in my brain. *I should be doing something I know how to do instead of pursuing a master's degree where the outcome is uncertain. Who knows if I'll even be able to earn a paycheck from this!*

I was feeling negative about myself. I remember kicking a door and slamming some plates on the table and yelling at David, who was two at the time, about something really unimportant. I remember thinking that my life being over might not be such a bad thing. Inside, I was seething with anger and self-hatred and berating myself with thoughts that I'd been stupid to choose this path.

Thank God I had enough Scripture in my head, like Romans 8:1: "For there is now no condemnation for those who are in Christ Jesus" (NIV) to realize all this self-slamming was not the way God saw me. Eventually I sat down at the kitchen table, put my head in my hands and meditated on this verse and others, praying for God's peace and perspective. I began to recognize the devil was involved, pouring gasoline on the fire with negative, self-defaming thoughts. I apologized to David and to God and focused on the domestic chore in front of me.

* * * *

Don't Flinch Now

* * * *

The drive to be "important" is very strong. The desire to do significant work is designed into me. And so I strive and slave and try to link what I do to something meaningful, permanent, and valuable.

When I fail to do that, I find myself at a crossroads. What's "important" in my life? Has it meant a forty-sixty hour a week job outside home with little thought of God's priorities? Has it been about satisfying the hopes and dreams of significant others while suppressing what I think God really wants? Has it been exclusively about the kids at the expense of other relationships God wants me to invest in?

Now is the time for honest evaluation. I dare not hold back; this is not the moment to hesitate. I need to ponder Caleb's counsel to Israel—take the land! But this is spiritual ground; the potential gain is even greater.

Who Am I Anyway?

I broke my glasses a couple years back. I tried to repair them on my own and botched the job. So I went to a one-hour eyeglass place and got new ones. This led me to a profound conclusion: I don't see very well without glasses.

In the physical realm, poor vision is resolved fairly quickly. Go to the optometrist, get an eye exam, get a new prescription then order the new glasses. In the personal realm it can take a lot more. I think I'm seeing things just fine, but really I'm blind as a bat without radar. Actually, I probably need more than new specs, I may need new eyes.

Up until the actual prospect of marriage, I tended to see my life as working hard at a job, serving within my Christian community, supporting a family, and being a good husband and father—a laudable vision. The prob-lem was the way I viewed success in each area. I still work hard, I still do ministry, I support my family, and I think I do a pretty fair job as a husband and dad. But how I do those things today is not the way I envisioned doing them at the beginning of married life.

• • • •

Taking chances

• • • •

The desire for adventure is strong in human beings. People explore this aspect of their personalities through different means—sky diving, exploring caves, racing a jet ski over a lake, blasting down the boulevard on a motorcycle, or bounding around the roof of a house putting up shingles. Some have turned their risk-taking bent into public service careers, such as police officers and firefighters. Men and women may also seek excitement through romantic involvements.

But how about in my spiritual life? Will I take risks with a comfortable part of my existence: say my career or my identity as a dad, to pursue a greater purpose for Jesus? I need to have eyes wide open for that kind of adventure.

Writing to the Ephesians, Paul notes:

> I pray also that the eyes of your heart may be enlightened in order that you may know the hope to which he has called you, the riches of his glorious inheritance in the saints, and his incomparably great power for us who believe.
>
> EPHESIANS 1:18–19A (NIV)

He asks that God would open the eyes of their hearts to a larger, more expansive reality. Paul was asking for an "ah-ha" experience for these Christians about their future, about the way God saw them, and the power available to them. He was asking for a grand illumination of the soul. People who've had their eyes opened to these truths are free to become spiritual risk-takers.

• • • •

Turkey Day Tumult

• • • •

Before I met Julia, I dated women who worked in jobs earning less than I. When we met, Julia was soon to become a full fledged doctor. She clearly had more earning potential than me.

This fact was humbling and the beginning of a soul-searching period. If I loved Julia and believed God brought her into my life, then what would I make of this strange combination of feelings: of attraction and dread, affection and self-protection. My old way of looking at myself and this new perspective God was trying to give me were at odds, resulting in a strange emotional double vision. My blurry perception was exposed when I proposed … for the first time.

During a Thanksgiving trip to Chicago, Julia and I visited the Museum of Science and Industry downtown. After touring the museum we crossed a footbridge over Lakeshore Drive to a little beach on Lake Michigan. It was chilly, but we wanted to see the lake, so we found a big rock to sit on. The idea started echoing in my head as we viewed the moonlit water, *what a romantic spot to pop the question*. I imagined the scene being one of those great stories to share with the kids someday. I hesitated a few minutes but eventually asked the big question to which Julia quickly replied, "Yes!"

In a movie there would have been squeals of jubilation, happy hugs, and smooches. Instead, I just sat there on the rock and offered a weak, "That's great." Julia picked up on my uncertainty. "What's wrong?" she asked, "You don't seem too sure about this." I admitted something was bugging me although I couldn't pin down the reasons. Graciously, Julia responded to my indecision by letting me off the hook. "You can ask me again sometime." We walked across the bridge to the parking lot, hand in hand. I went from single, to engaged, to single again all in a half-hour.

The reason for my doubts? Concerns that Julia's earning power would give her "the power" in our marriage and that she would have the last say in all the important decisions. My old vision for "being the man" wouldn't allow me to express those fears. It was wimpy! But God was challenging me to be forthright with Julia. Could I see myself as a person of value because of Christ's acceptance and be honest about my concerns, or would the old way of looking at myself win out?

Thank God, the new vision finally came into focus, and we had the discussion about money and power. Julia listened as I voiced my apprehension, although there was no basis for this fear. Julia had never gained her sense of self from how much money she made and would not use her income as leverage in our marriage. She never has.

But once this concern was faced, with the help of my new eyes in Christ, I felt comfortable asking her to marry me again. This time I asked her in the very unromantic atmosphere of a small apartment watching a football game on TV on Christmas Eve. She accepted, and we married the following September.

. . . .

Promise or Peril

. . . .

Being a spiritual frontiersman is not much different than being a frontiersman in any age. Frontiersmen (or frontier women) have a willingness to go places other people might not go because there's danger, discomfort, and uncertainty. But a frontiersman has the vision to see great opportunity where others see dim prospects, adventure where others see peril, life where others see death.

Becoming a spiritual risk taker doesn't mean staking out a claim on new land but staking my future on what God has given me, on the fact that God is good and his promises are worth trusting. It requires seeing life as it could be but believing it's already a done deal. I just need to believe and act. It may mean decisions that cause others to question my sanity because I'm banking on the unseen.

For me, one of the earliest issues was my view of significance, which was closely related to earning power. God wanted me to place that vision of myself in his hands and begin to realize in a deeper way that significance starts with my relationship with him and continues as I carry out the orders he gives me.

The Christian's identity as a loved, accepted, totally forgiven person is a well-known truth, preached in churches throughout the world. However, believing these truths when there's something at stake, like the way I prefer to think about myself, is something else. My marriage was an early fulcrum for this growth point.

For others it may be something else. Kris may be

a person who tells other people what to do; she runs the show. Other people count on her to say how things should be. But putting it on the line for Jesus may mean relinquishing that level of responsibility for a while. She may seek a job which demands less of her so she has more time and energy for God's purposes outside the nine to five.

Perhaps Jonas is the hotshot salesperson who brings in the biggest accounts. Because he's chosen to spend more time with the home-building ministry or help out his sick and aging parents he may not earn "Salesperson of the Year" honors. In fact, he might end up middle-of-the-pack in sales figures. Even though he's still doing a good job and working hard, his manager begins to question Jonas' "passion" for the job. His status on the sales team declines.

Some people gain a lot of meaning from being the go-to person at home, the one who makes the cogs turn, sets the social schedule, packs the lunches, and helps the kids with homework. But maybe there's something else God wants mom to do— hang out more with neighbors and friends who don't know God, tutor other people's kids and not just her own, counsel a younger person trying to figure out how to make a happy marriage. Is she willing to trade her identity as the domestic go-to person to become God's go-to person?

•   •   •   •

A Changing Vision

•   •   •   •

Pursuing God's larger purpose stimulates tension: a good tension, but tension none-the-less. It's a tension between the way I like to see myself and the way God wants me to be. If I go after his bigger purpose and refuse to turn my gaze from it, I'll discover that my eyes are now wide open in a way they've never been before. And here's what I'll notice:

Sense of value. It does not come from my paycheck, how I'm perceived at my job, at home, or in the neighborhood. According to the Bible, if I have accepted God's gift of forgiveness through Jesus Christ, I'm a new person. "Therefore, if anyone is in Christ, he is a new creation; the old has gone, the new has come!" (2 Corinthians 5:17, NIV). Also because of this, God has accepted me as his child. He is committed to loving me forever, and he has a plan for my life that I am exclusively blueprinted to carry out, i.e. Ephesians 2:10, "For we are God's workmanship, created in Christ Jesus to do good works, which God prepared in advance for us to do" (NIV).

Now, that all sounds great in theory, but making decisions to follow the Lord that puts these truths to the test will transform me and the way I think. As I choose to believe God's view of my worth, it will reshape the way I feel and think. Instead of having that walking-on-gelatin feeling that I experience from trying to gain approval from others, I'll notice a strength developing in me that supersedes any manmade criteria for value. It is the difference between building my house on rock or on sand.

Meaning and purpose. Now, from God's point of view, the most important thing in this life is not whether I have a public park or the wing of a church named after me someday. A newspaper friend wanted a building named after himself in his hometown. It doesn't come from having a string of letters after my name either—M.A., M.B.A., Ph.D. Nothing wrong with degrees; I have a couple.

My satisfaction will not come from fame or acknowledgement as a great person in my community or at my job or from being a great church leader or having all the kids get college degrees. Am I carrying out God's plan for my life, which may or may not include fame, fortune, or accolades?

So, for me, watching my kids, working on a variety of freelance magazine projects, doing evangelism and discipleship, and caring for people who come to our home Bible study is all part of my design. Loving Julia, who is also uniquely designed and crafted by God, is something I'm suited for too. My meaning and purpose will come as I follow his lead about what I ought to do and who I ought to be.

Think about what Jesus says in John 13, after getting up from dinner to wash the grimy, smelly feet of his disciples:

> You call me "Teacher" and "Lord," and rightly so, for that is what I am. Now that I, your Lord and Teacher, have washed your feet, you also should wash one another's feet. I have set you an example that you should do as I have done for you. I tell you the truth, no servant is greater than his master, nor is a messenger greater than the one who sent him. Now that you know these things, you will be blessed if you do them.
>
> JOHN 13:13–17 (NIV)

What is Jesus saying? Learning to be a servant of others, in the same way that Christ has served me, will lead to the real fulfillment I long for. This is the meaning of verse 17. The word *blessed* is the Greek word *makarios*, which has the larger meaning of satisfaction and happiness from being in the center of God's will.

For Jesus, it didn't come from being called "Teacher" or "Lord" but from loving others sacrificially and loving the Father wholeheartedly. Am I pursuing this kind of life? I need to start asking Christ how he wants me to give my life away and thereby experience my God-given destiny.

Without this mindset, I never would have known the satisfaction of spending time with a friend waiting for his dad to come out of surgery, being with my wife through labor, explaining the meaning of the cross to a bunch of junior high kids, or helping a very confused and immature guy meet Christ. I've missed opportunities too—not helping a stranded person on the roadside, cutting short a conversation with a person in need, acting like I wasn't at home when the phone rang. But I'm glad for every time I've done what Jesus said. And it's changed my life into something grander and better than it would have been.

Integration. The question that ought to guide my thinking about life is whether I'm pleasing to the Lord who loved me and saved me. Am I acting in accordance with his love for me and my love for him? Is my life more and more integrated with these truths? To say "I love the Lord" but then not seek him or try to understand the ways he wants me to change results in an odd disconnect. The Holy Spirit is cut off from bringing more and more of God's love into my heart and filling my life with God-centered meaning.

But if I see myself trying to live in accordance with God's love and direction, I will have a sense of increasing personal wholeness, which is very gratifying and motivating. I remember looking at people who could laugh easily at themselves and with others. I wondered if I could ever be that well connected emotionally. I was too concerned about the way I looked in the eyes of others to be that vulnerable and "silly." I can say that God has changed me to a high degree as I've continued trying to live a life that's focused on him and loving others. There's still a long way to go but I've changed in ways that I longed for years to see.

Freedom. If my intrinsic value is as a child of God, then what someone else thinks just doesn't really matter in the long run. Jesus was such a master of this. As John writes in the second chapter of his Gospel,

> Now while he was in Jerusalem at the Passover Feast, many people saw the miraculous signs he was doing and believed in his name. But Jesus would not entrust himself to them, for he knew all men. He did not need man's testimony about man, for he knew what was in a man.
>
> JOHN 2:23–25 (NIV)

Jesus did not bank on the opinion of others to shape the way he should think about himself. He was the ultimate free person.

There have been plenty of moments, hours, and days when I've chosen the world's standard of evaluation over God's. But there have been amazing benchmark moments when I've seen myself as a loved and accepted person by God. The liberation is intoxicating. It's like free-falling from 30,000 feet, confident in your parachute and your ability to land. You're wide open emotionally, fearless to experience the force of the atmosphere on your skin, the dazzling color of the sky, the scope of creation below. Yeah, it's that good. Once you've known it, you want more.

Rich relationships. Once I'm okay with where my value comes from, I'm free to build friendships with people whom God wants me to bond with. The freedom that comes from knowing who you are as God's man or woman will lead you into relationships you probably never imagined. You become open to depths of friendship you could only hope for. Following God's lead into relationships is kind of like a divine treasure hunt, where joy is located in places you never would have expected.

For example, one of the most joyous times in my life came from pretending to be a pirate with my oldest son when he was only four or five. We dressed up using whatever props we could find, and then ran out to our gym set which magically transformed into a buccaneer's sloop. Just a few years before I probably would not have done something so "childish" in the eyes of the world, but spending time with my son meant "washing his feet" this way. I joined in his imaginative play, linking with him in a personal way, which was richly rewarding for both of us.

Transparency. Even if they can't express themselves this way, most people appreciate someone who talks freely about his or her faults, problems, and struggles. Being free in the Lord gives me the power to do that. I can be my funny, thoughtful, or doubtful self, and people will either become curious or walk away scratching their heads. It's like Paul's comment in 2 Corinthians 4:7, "But we have this treasure in jars of clay to show that this all-surpassing power is from God and not from us" (NIV). It takes God to make my fractured jar of a life into something intriguing to others. But that's what he does.

What Will It Cost Me?

I don't like to think about costs. Especially as an American, I live in a "cost" vacuum; I prefer to think about life in terms of choices, alternatives and opportunities. But every choice I make involves deciding against other options. For example, the choice to have dinner out involves the decision not to use that forty to sixty dollars on something else. I could go out to the movies with that money, or give it to charity or buy forty to sixty items at the local dollar discount store.

There will be costs associated with doing what God wants me to do. Yes, the costs are worth it, because of the great pay-off spiritually, now and for all time. As Paul writes to the Galatians in chapter six, when I use time, money, and other resources at the discretion of the Holy Spirit, there will be a corresponding spiritual harvest, including a quality of life which he describes as "eternal." That's a heavenly peace, hope, purpose, and joy today that nothing in this world can provide. As Jesus explained, "I have come that they may have life, and have it to the full." (John 10:10, NIV)

But the costs of following God are not the same as the straight-line costs involved in other choices. If I choose DSL instead of dial-up I'll pay more, but go faster on the Internet. That's clear and true for all who make that choice. The costs of trading in my current life and identity will vary based on the unique guidance the Lord is giving me. It might mean a lower paying job. The primary cost could be my significance in the eyes of people important to me.

This schematic may help you sort out the cost of following the Lord in your life. I've included a made-up situation to give you something to think about:

- Calling: get more involved in the kids' spiritual, moral, and personal development
- Solution: spend more time with the kids teaching and modeling a relationship with God
- Adjustment: work part-time from home

Personal Costs:
1. Won't have as much adult interaction, which I value
2. Should spend more time learning and thinking about what's influencing the kids at the expense of pursuing my own interests

Financial Costs:
1. Will mean a decrease in total family income of $20,000 a year

Status:

1. May suffer in the eyes of my peers because won't be seen as the "team player" I once was

2. May suffer in the eyes of my boss who may not see me as the ladder climber I have been, resulting in lost opportunity for promotions

This example is not exhaustive, but is meant to clarify how a person will need to approach this very important step of altering his life. But isn't cost counting anti-Christian? Doesn't it show a lack of trust in God to take care of me? No, not at all. This kind of decision is ultimately one of increased discipleship. Jesus used the most bracing language and examples possible to make sure his followers understood what this would mean. Look at Luke 14 for a moment:

> Whoever does not carry his own cross and come after me cannot be my disciple. For which one of you, when he wants to build a tower, does not first sit down and calculate the cost to see if he has enough to complete it? Otherwise, when he has laid a foundation and is not able to finish, all who observe it begin to ridicule him, saying, "This man began to build and was not able to finish."
>
> LUKE 14:27–30 (NIV)

The context of this parable is discipleship the way Jesus presented it: all out. Jesus says I should consider what it might mean to do this, because if I don't and I find the choice I've made too "expensive" then I'll bail out. That's bad enough, but worse from the parable's standpoint is the response of others who watch me bail out—"This guy couldn't finish what he started." When you veer from the path you've been on, you get an initial reaction, from polite atta-boys to plainspoken derision. But there's another part—those same people who congratulate you or shake their heads will watch you, some of them quite closely.

Believers who jump into a life-changing reality without estimating the consequences risk becoming "flavorless salt" as Jesus explains a few verses later: "If even salt has become tasteless, with what will it be seasoned? It is useless either for the soil or for the manure pile; it is thrown out. (Luke 34–35, NIV)" He's not talking about my relationship with the Father, but what happened to flavorless salt, at least in that day.

This doesn't mean that God won't work with false starts or miscalculations. Look at Peter! God is all about second and third and fourth chances. But I should understand that my decision for God bears great weight in the larger picture of what he's doing in the world. So I need to count those costs!

• • • •

Getting Real about Costs

• • • •

It's easy to discuss "cost" in a clinical, disconnected way, but every sacrifice I ponder, related to pursuing Jesus, will have a very connected, tangible, emotional edge.

Julia and I were having dinner with several other couples when this book came up. The discussion turned rather intense; I didn't really expect that. But I guess I learned a new cost of creating this manuscript. As we talked about what it would mean to downsize or transform your life to be more available to God, the conversation turned to salary. The comment that echoed most was this honest and revealing statement from one friend, "I like having the things that my income allows me to have."

One of the costs of following Jesus may indeed be financial. During the course of my life I've never made more than $25,000 a year. And that's on the high side. Some years I've made $10,000, other years only a couple thousand bucks. At the beginning I struggled with questions about my value or whether my life was really adding up in any important way related to the paycheck question. And I've been on salary calculators and realized that folks with my level of experience and knowledge can make much more than I do.

It goes back to where I get my value—do I see myself as inherently valuable as a child of God or is it all linked to how much money I bring in or my career stats. It's a full-bodied question and not one I raise lightly. Personal worth and where I derive mine from is an intense issue, for men and women.

Women also have the extra challenge of their self-assessment coming from relationships, which is a whole other Pandora's box: "Am I a good wife? Am I a good daughter? Am I a good friend?" For guys, those questions don't seem to have as much effect on our self esteem, although they exist. But for moms feeling drawn to work or volunteer activities outside the home, one of the looming, perhaps scary, questions they'll face will be, "Am I a good parent?" This is especially difficult as they conclude that one of the biggest roadblocks to greater spiritual usefulness is the time spent carting Junior around to select sports, martial arts classes, and after-school robots club. Making a decision to limit children's activities *may be* the key that unlocks your schedule for God. This will be swimming upstream.

I thank God that he has given me a measure of peace on my personal worth. I see my current status—low contribution on the money side, high on the ministry and home life side—as part of God's plan. Even still, I occasionally revisit the question of whether I will continue to play out this hand or dump it in favor of something that looks better. That's an ongoing struggle. I can't say I've got it licked, although I think I've gained a fair amount of resolve. There is a way—that I don't fully understand—in which God is using my faithfulness to this particular call in this phase of my life to advance his goals.

I have to ask myself, regularly, am I seeking what's good for me or what's best in God's plan? There's the tough question. I consider Ephesians 2:10 an important verse in sorting this out. That's the verse that says I am God's workmanship, created in Christ Jesus to do good works, which God prepared in advance for me to do. This verse doesn't specify the good works; it just says "good works." I try to picture it in military terms— manning my particular outpost in God's plan, doing the good works he wants me to, within the community he wants me to do them in, taking spiritual ground he wants me to take.

My situation is part of a spiritual mission that causes me to think twice about making sudden changes. Could I jump out of this current spot into something else? Yes. But would this new arrangement be the thing God wants me to do? Maybe not. Could he work through a new situation? Of course, he's God. He can do whatever he wants. This isn't an anxiety-filled search for the perfect will of God. But if I desire God's best I'll check the road signs (circumstances, Spirit's leadings, confirmation from uninfluenced sources outside of myself), consult the map (the Bible), talk with fellow travelers, and confer with the Highway Engineer.

This goes back to my view of earthly and spiritual life. I like to think of Revelation, especially from chapter four onward, as a heavenly view of earthly events. For instance, Revelation 12:1–6 is a symbolic stage play of the events surrounding the birth of Christ. I have a different perspective. According to Revelations 4:1, John was summoned to heaven and shown the wondrous things described. I think Revelations 12:1–6 is the heavenly view on the Christmas story, a narrative familiar to even the biblically illiterate—Joseph and Mary, tired from their journey, can't find a room in crowded Bethlehem, but an innkeeper provides accommodations in his stable, where Mary gives birth. King Herod is disturbed about the news, given to him by the Magi that another king has been born, and he orders the annihilation of the Bethlehem boys. Joseph, warned in a dream, takes his young wife and son and escapes to Egypt before the massacre.

But that's not the view from heaven, because God sees the scene as it actually is, from the spiritual point of view. This wasn't just Herod brutally murdering innocent toddlers, but Satan himself i.e. "the dragon" of Revelations 12:4, acting through the paranoid king to destroy the Messiah. Why am I bringing this up? Because my decisions have a spiritual dimension to them, which is of no less value, even though they may seem mundane and unimportant from an earthly viewpoint.

But incredible things are unfolding in the invisible realm of angels and demons because of those decisions:

the alignment of spiritual troops because of where I've decided to work; the commitment of resources to protect spiritual seed planted through a conversation at the park; the application of the Spirit's convicting power to another's heart because my kids were respectful and real at a restaurant; the opening of unseen doors for the Gospel since I increased my giving to missions.

• • • •

Useful Stuff vs. Perfect Stuff

• • • •

I like to have nice stuff; who doesn't? How many people are willing to work themselves to death in order to have the nice stuff? Many are. But being available for God's purposes may mean keeping the "worn out" living room furniture, not redecorating the dining room, not putting in a new kitchen, using my mother-in-law's forks and spoons, and buying used instead of new as a rule.

How many folks really *need* a satellite dish, a plasma screen TV, high speed internet, etc. I don't need it but I like to have it. And I can afford it. How about that clothing budget—$500 a year, $1000 a year, $2000? Have I exchanged my living room furniture in the last two years just because I was getting tired of the 'old stuff,' even though the old stuff was still quite usable?

Following God in the area of availability may mean exposing the stuff I have to greater use and abuse. I offer Proverbs 14:4 as exhibit A, "Where no oxen are, the manger is clean, but much revenue comes by the strength of the ox" (NAS). Here's how I take this: You can keep your "manger" clean (or your crib, your abode, your castle—choose a metaphor) by not populating it with a messy ox—or messy kids, or messy people.

But, there's also no "revenue." The NIV translates the last part of Proverbs 14:4, "but from the strength of an ox comes an abundant harvest." People are the harvest I should be concerned about as a Christian. Are people—friends, neighbors, co-workers, our kids' classmates, their parents—being affected for God through the use of my resources? Even if I'm not able to replace those resources in the manner I'm use to because I'm not making the money I use to make?

There are times when I wish Julia and I didn't have so many "oxen." Even without opening our home to others, we have six people, one dog, two cats, and one bird inhabiting our house almost constantly.

Our dog Molly use to have an occasional bladder-control incident. I would get really frustrated, especially if I had recently shampooed the carpet and we were expecting guests. That could drive me crazy! On the flip side, even with the clean-ups, we benefited by having a family pet we loved and visitors enjoyed. When we had to put her to sleep because of cancer, many people told us how sorry they were. A friend said she cried about Molly. She was part of our family and our ministry.

If I keep following the Lord into the area of hospitality, which 1 Peter 4:9 commands for all Christians, then I'll find myself spending money in areas I would not have imagined.

Doug Patch, coordinator of adult ministries at Xenos Christian Fellowship in Columbus, OH, hosts a small group Bible study, although "small" may be a poor descriptor. Doug and wife Chris usually welcome between twenty and thirty people every other Tuesday night into their home. They have Bible study in the basement, a 540-square-foot space that requires an especially low thermostat to make things bearable in the summer.

"If we wait until getting home from work—a couple hours before the meeting—to turn it down, the air conditioning just can't catch up in the heat of the day," Doug noted. "Plus, what's key is getting furniture, walls, and carpet cool, not just the air."

Doug describes himself as a "very conscientious guy about utility costs." "You might think this drives me crazy but I have so prioritized the comfort of the guest that I want nothing in our control to detract from peoples' experience and ability to hear the message." So Doug and his wife Chris intentionally allot extra money in their budget for electricity expenses. Some might call him misguided; Jesus would not. As Jesus advises in Luke 16:9, "I tell you, use worldly wealth to gain friends for yourselves, so that when it is gone, you will be welcomed into eternal dwellings" (NIV).

•　•　•　•

Time and Status

•　•　•　•

Maybe I'm not really hung up about my stuff. That's great. How about my time? In making some life adjustments, I may already have thought out ways I want to spend the time dividend, which may include some very good things—volunteering, discipleship, spending time with the kids, and church ministry. I may also hope to use the extra hours for hobbies—playing golf, fishing, working out, painting, or quilting. God's question may be, "Will you give that over to me?"

If I've already walked through deeper trust issues to make the changes I've made, having God ask this question may seem too much. But is it too much? And can I trust him even more deeply with the use of my time? I discuss it further in chapter ten, but the dreams I have for my home life may not correspond with the vision God has. His vision is better!

Then there's the status factor. I can give up things; I'm not a materialist. I can grant God my time and ask him to teach me how to use it. But having people consider me incompetent or wasteful of my life—that's the left hook that really hurts.

I ran into an old high school teacher many years ago, a man whom I respect and who was very helpful to me at an important point in my life. When I told him I'd decided to be a journalist, he hung his head. I could tell he was disappointed. I suppose he imagined I'd become a big business hotshot, maybe a CEO. He had left teaching and done well in business himself. I walked away from that brief encounter feeling a bit depressed, feeling as if I'd let him down, although I'm confident about my life.

Doug Patch's decision to take on ministry, professionally and as a lifestyle, was a "step back" in the eyes of some. He was a trainer and physical therapist for world-class divers and track and field athletes. He was head trainer for the 1986 Goodwill Games in Moscow, where he worked with Carl Lewis, Jackie Joyner-Kersee and other "are-you-kidding-he-knows-those-people" names in the world of sports. He observes:

> I walked in opening ceremonies in the U.S. track and field parade uniform with Carl, Jackie and others. I spent three weeks taking part in thrilling events before 105,000 spectators, including then U.S.S.R. President Mikhail Gorbachev. I helped Carl and Jackie and others with injuries.

But as I was flying home from Moscow trying to re-create the excitement in my head I realized there was something even more exciting going on. The Lord was allowing me to help this new Christian, Donal O'Mathuna, grow in his faith. The importance of that one work superseding all the things I had accomplished was crystal clear.

I knew there was nothing wrong morally with my involvement with the team, but I was doing it for *my* thrill, *my* buzz and *my* ego. The cost was three weeks of my life, coming home fatigued beyond belief and being less in touch with my wife and people in our church. It was time to quit.

Doug also noted that his decision not to join the track and field team for the 1987 World Indoor Track Championships ticked off a few folks. "My 'turn down' in 1987 was only a week or so before the event because I had just gotten accepted into seminary and it was the first week of class," he said. He was invited to join the team for the 1988 Summer Olympics in Seoul, South Korea, but also declined. That's the last time he heard from someone at U.S. Track and Field about a job.

As I've pursued my relationship with God, based on the truth of Scripture versus my circumstances, feelings, or the opinion of others, I've noticed the Holy Spirit buoying my spirit. He carries me along and lifts me up and helps me see that I'm part of this massive project called "the church" which will be revealed for what it really is someday—like a picture from Revelation—but for now is something that I don't fully comprehend. I've had times like Doug experienced on his flight home when God revealed to me in a very personal way that his big project is more meaningful than any byline I'll get published. The cost of not being on top in my career will begin to fade in the shadow of this growing truth.

But these feelings don't stop with career. Full-time or part-time caregivers face an equally tempting replacement for godly goals. Many moms, and some dads, apply all the energy they would expend on career achievement on school or extra-curricular volunteerism. While serving in my child's school is admirable and may indeed be the way God wants to use me right now, I should ask God to show me if that's the case. Serving as the PTO president, running my kid's scout troop and coordinating the soccer team snack *might* be more about my own ego than connecting with people for God's sake.

Would I study the Bible with a friend on Tuesday morning if it meant accepting a smaller role at my child's school? Could I re-allocate my schedule to pray for teachers and administrators, even though it's an activity that will never earn me public kudos? Of course, God may reveal that I'm exactly in the place he wants me, doing what he wants me to do, *for now*. However, I need to stay open to how he may lead tomorrow or next week. The situation may need to change. This is part of staying in step with the Spirit (see Galatians 5:25).

This can sound strange, perhaps other-worldly. Well, it is from another world, in the most positive sense. Consider Jesus' final long prayer before his arrest,

> I am coming to you now, but I say these things while I am still in the world, so that they may have the full measure of my joy within them. I have given them your word and the world has hated them, for they are not of the world any more than I am of the world.
>
> JOHN 17:13–14 (NIV)

God's truth will transform me into someone the world doesn't quite get, and in some cases, hates. Yet his word also produces inexplicable joy. This is the glorious absurdity of the Christian life—that which provides meaning and satisfaction also puts me at odds with values I once cherished and which are still cherished by people around me. But I'm not of this world any longer so I should live accordingly.

As I begin pursuing God's goals I'll become less worried about having concrete milestones that mark my life as "important." God takes care of that. As Paul points out,

> I care very little if I am judged by you or by any human court; indeed, I do not even judge myself. My conscience is clear, but that does not make me innocent. It is the Lord who judges me.
>
> 1 CORINTHIANS 4:2–4 (NIV)

Now there's freedom. What if I was just a little bit less worried about how I'm stacking up against societal norms or the expectations of significant people? Where I'm satisfied living within my means, instead of constantly fretting and banging my head about whether I have the latest gadgets or nice clothing or the perfect house? If I commit myself to God's main purposes the costs won't seem so costly. Living near God's heart will become more valuable than what I've left behind.

How Will I Get There?

If you've made the decision to give your identity as a professional, parent, or student over to God and said to him, "Use me, change me, make me the person you want me to be" then you've already made a giant stride on your way to greatness. You've looked at yourself in the mirror and found the reflection lacking, but instead of stuffing your findings in a dusty file drawer in the back of your mind, you've turned to Christ. Excellent. Now what?

Well, certainly what God will tell you now is something figured out through a lot of prayer and a lot of counsel. You would make a mistake to assume that tomorrow you should go to your boss, hand in the two-week notice, and brush the envelope dust off your hands. Or that you should announce to your college professor, "I now realize that differential equations are irrelevant to the larger call of the Lord so I won't be taking today's mid-term."

I'd like to recommend an exercise I've given to prospective newlyweds, which I'll include here. Some of this is borrowed material from other sources, notably a worksheet put together by a Christian brother, Mark Bair. If you're married, do this exercise with your spouse. Do it separately before coming together to discuss your thoughts.

• • • •

Shared Vision Exercise

• • • •

First, write a mission statement for your life. For example, you might write, "To reflect God's love in every role that I play in life as a parent, employee, supervisor, son, brother, and neighbor."

Second, how does the mission statement you wrote stack up with the biblical position about a Christian's mission? Check Matthew 28:18–20; Mark 10:45; 1 John 3:16.

Third, where do you see your life five and ten years from now?

This question has several components:

1. What factors are *likely* to be definite in your life five and ten years from now? Write these down using simple declarative sentences, i.e. I'll be thirty-three or thirty-eight; my parents will be in their fifties, sixties, etc.; the children will be eight or ten, going to school; I'll be done with school; I will have worked at the same place ten years, etc.

2. Think about where you'd like to be in five and ten

years, as a spiritual person? This question is meant to help you spell out an immediate vision for carrying out the mission. When thinking about this, think in terms of the three main areas—service to others, knowledge and use of the Bible, and personal growth. These areas also include: service to others especially believers in your small group community, discipleship, and evangelism; personal growth, through prayer, a dependence on God in trials and difficulties, giving of money, and how to work with the Lord on sin issues and areas of weakness. Write statements such as, "I would like to know more of the Bible and be able to refer to it from memory; I would like to be a more patient person; etc."

3. Think about other desires you have for your life - career, financial, family. Sometimes there's conflict between spiritual goals and other types of goals. Remember, holding a job, earning an income, and having a family all fit within God's will. In fact, the Bible has much to say about the value of each of these, but all in terms of how they fit under the umbrella of commitment to Christ. Spell out your hopes in these other areas for five and ten years from now.

4. Now, for couples, come together and compare notes. Note what things are similar and what things are different. Especially talk about your mission statements. Checkmark the areas where some discussion needs to happen. A couple's vision has to incorporate the hopes and aspirations of both sides, not a tacit signing on of one person to the other's vision.

Shared vision will lead to the greatest good done in God's plan, as you pool resources toward a common mission and goals.

5. For singles, get together with another single and discuss what you came up with. This exercise is important in helping you determine your life direction. The Bible is clear that singleness is a gift, not a liability. However, if God should bring someone into your life, this exercise will help you know if that person is on the same page with you. And, once you've sorted things out about God's purpose for you, you can begin praying God will bring someone of like mind along. You might meet a great Christian single, but if he/she is committed to inner city ministry while you see yourself heading for Southeast Asia as a missionary, you might not be suited for each other.

So now you have a mission statement for your life. That's wonderful. What kind of vision do you have? This will affect the decisions you make as they relate to the rest of this chapter.

Let's consider the example of Rita. She's decided that her mission has to do with kids and being used in the lives of children as a teacher and administrator. That's the big picture. Right now, she's sensing God's pull toward leading the children's program for her small to mid-sized congregation, which is a volunteer position, not paid.

How much time will this take? We'll play this conservatively and imagine it will require four to six hours each Sunday. And let's throw in some meetings at the church and phone calling to round up volunteers plus planning for special kids' events. We'll estimate it takes another fifteen to twenty hours during the week. This will fluctuate depending on time of year, but in general this should work.

Obviously, with that kind of commitment during the week, something will have to change. As Rita pushes forward on this endeavor, she notices this commitment eats up quite a bit of family time. Maybe she needs to look at altering her job or making adjustments to other volunteer opportunities.

Presently Rita works forty to fifty hours a week as a loan officer. She likes her job. She likes helping young people get their first home loan, or helping a financially strapped family get a consolidation loan. Her job gives her contact with different people in the community, and while she sees God pulling her more toward youth work, she senses from the Spirit a value in having this larger connection to her area. She's actually worked with individuals who come to her church and had the opportunity to tell other customers about her faith.

So what should she do? Rita could look into going part-time at her job, even though that will cut her chances at a supervisor's spot in the future. Perhaps she could job share with someone else. If she's in a place where she can rely on benefits from her husband, perhaps she could offer that as a carrot to her employer. So instead of the forty-five to fifty-five hours she now clocks, she could work an almost-full-time job of thirty to thirty-five hours a week. Or Maybe Rita could rearrange her hours, from nine hours, five days a week, to ten on three days and five hours on two days.

When it comes to God the options are dizzying. But it starts with prayerfully, studiously, humbly seeking His leading about your mission and the vision he's directing you to pursue. You need to ask him sincerely what your life should be about. You should pray about that for the next seven days. And if you're still not clear, pray another seven days. You should talk about your efforts to scope out a mission and vision with another believer who's trying earnestly to follow Jesus. That should be followed by asking for their prayer-fed and Spirit-guided understanding and perceptions about who you are now and what you should be about.

The many ways this can play out are as vast as the thoughts of God. But it starts with the mission. Let's consider Alex. He may land on the fact God wants him to spend more time building relationships with people at work. He determines, through prayer and counsel from his wife and believing friends, that eating in the lunchroom is one way to get that done. He asks God to prompt him about which co-workers to eat with. Alex also decides to join the company softball team. He sees the team as a way to spend time with co-workers in a more relaxed setting where casual conversation might happen.

Now, what has Alex done with his current job? Not much, except rearrange the current schedule so he's more available to God's purposes.

What kind of things might you do to fulfill God's plan for your life? Here are a few possibilities:

Volunteer at work. You may sense God wanting you involved with co-workers more, as cited above, but that you need to get out of your cubicle and serve. So maybe you sign up to be on the blood drive committee. Or agree to coordinate the annual holiday party. Or sign up for the corporate team that's participating in your town's business Olympics, featuring such renowned athletic challenges as the egg toss, the three-legged race and the tug-o-war.

Volunteering for anything will set you apart anyway. The U.S. Bureau of Labor Statistics reported that around three in ten Americans volunteered in 2005, numbers that had remained unchanged from the previous two years. Doing unpaid work for the sake of a good cause, at work or elsewhere, earns respect in the eyes of co-workers, neighbors, fellow soccer moms, and classmates, as long as you approach it with modesty and sincerity (see Philippians 2:3–4). Volunteering is only a logical response to God's many gifts to us.

Work at a company because of ministry or the chance to make relationships, rather than the measure of my paycheck. Zach could very well make more money somewhere else. But, because he's given God his career, he now sees that where he's employed is the right work to do, even though he could earn a better paycheck at a different company.

But Zach has determined he should be where he is because of Andy, who he's been friends with but who has just recently taken an interest in spiritual things. Zach and Andy have begun studying the Bible once a week at lunch, and they end up talking about Jesus and faith in God during coffee breaks. God also seems to be generating curiosity in Al, who works in another department, but whom Zach sees in the lunchroom. So, till further notice, Zach is not going anywhere, because his present job has him laboring beside some folks who are responding to God.

As a job seeker, you will most likely *not* have the tangible reasons listed above for wanting to work somewhere. You may be re-entering the job market or seeking that first job. You will need to research the companies in your field, but with a God track in mind as well as a career track. What companies have policies that permit workers to hold Bible studies or prayer times during lunch? Which business offers the most schedule flexibility so you can still help out with that inner city after-school tutoring program? Or coach your daughter's soccer team? My decisions should be based on opportunity for spiritual revenue more than net take-home.

Work at a job because it allows me to be more available outside work. After working through the mission and vision exercise, let's say you've decided you want to help lead a home group Bible study that will be the starting place for other similar groups. Your current employer expects you to work on weekends, when the group would meet. But you've heard of a position at another company, which offers more scheduling options. You have a friend who works there who's also leading home Bible studies and he affirms this other company is very adaptable as long as you work hard and meet expectations when you're there. You leave your old employer, even though it offers greater "growth" possibilities for your career, and take the job at the other place. Misguided? From the world's view, yes, most certainly. From God's? Look at Matthew 19 for a second:

> And everyone who has left houses or brothers or sisters or father or mother or children or fields for my sake will receive a hundred times as much and will inherit eternal life. But many who are first will be last, and many who are last will be first.
>
> MATTHEW 19:29–30 (NIV)

In this regard, God isn't even asking me to leave my house or family. But he is asking for my "field." In a first century, agrarian context the "field" represented a primary means for making a living. Will I leave my field for the fields of God?

Choose a vocation for the sake of God's call over prestige. Some have chosen careers that are low prestige in the eyes of society, or at least their peers, because God wants them to serve a certain community or use their skills with a certain population. In some cases he may use their experience to prepare them for other kinds of service.

My friend Lynne has a son Josh. Josh intends to use his newly minted medical degree and do something really wild—become a missionary doctor. What kind of money will he make? Very little in comparison with the average U.S. salary. But this is his dream, his calling, and his path.

I worked for a while at a chain of community newspapers. I started out as a beat writer for the *New Carlisle Sun*, a weekly publication for a network of small towns and farming communities north of Dayton, Ohio. I liked the *New Carlisle Sun*. I took photos of kids; I wrote stories about science fairs and school board meetings; I got to know the people.

I worked there for one and a half years and remember people asking me, "So, when are you moving on?" I don't have a problem with moving on. There's a time for that. But I felt like God had placed me there for a time. Perhaps it was too long in the eyes of some. But there was a landmark moment in my experience there.

During my stint in New Carlisle I was contacted about a job at a small daily paper. It was a step up, a way to put a little zing in my career. But I struggled with the decision, even though I wasn't sure why. I even panicked about it one night, breaking out in cold sweats and breathing rapidly like the churning of a locomotive's wheels. I called a doctor fearing a heart attack. The nurse on the other end encouraged me to breathe into a brown paper bag. I slowly regained composure and developed a renewed respect for lunch sacks.

In the midst of this decision-making dilemma, God gave me a word. I've never understood very well this idea that God would give someone a "word of knowledge'" as I've heard it called. But I think that's what happened.

And that word was … *blastus*—yes, *blastus*. What or who or why is a blastus? I didn't know either. This word kept echoing in my head, like an annoying song you can't forget. I decided to look it up in the Bible. Hey, there was a guy named Blastus in the New Testament. Fantastic! He was an aide to King Herod, listed in Acts 12. Right before Herod's guts burst open. All right, interesting, not sure what it has to do with journalism, but okay.

Then I felt the Spirit saying, "Look at the dictionary." So I did. And there it was again, this crazy, meaningless sound that had been pinging like a distress beacon in my head for a week. And I learned that I had spelled it wrong. It was *blastos* not *blastus*. I learned it was a Greek word, meaning germ or sprout. And there you go. God was telling me I was a germ. Whoa!

I settled on the sprout idea. And here's the interpretation the Lord provided: at that point in my writing career I was merely a sprout. My job at the *Sun* was allowing me to grow in a safe, secure environment and I shouldn't try to push that along too quickly by transplanting myself to another paper. So I stayed at the *Sun* and in the sun, with the Son. Eventually I did transplant, but after I had become something a little hardier than a sprout.

God may want me to stay somewhere because he's grooming me for something else even though a career counselor might say, "Go for it!" I should be willing to wait and serve him patiently where I'm at. In this respect, the parable of the talents applies:

> Well done, good and faithful servant! You have been faithful with a few things; I will put you in charge of many things. Come and share your master's happiness!
>
> MATTHEW 25:21, 23 (NIV)

Go to work for myself. Some have concluded this is God's course for their lives, so they might be available to him in some greater way with their time and energy. These are people who may or may not have an entrepreneurial bone or muscle in them. But they're stepping out into a whole new world of endeavor out of a desire to know and love Christ better.

Give up my income. Maybe I can do just fine on the income of my spouse and God wants me to do some other things instead of make money at a job. He still has work for me to do, but not the kind that will earn remuneration.

My friend Betty Carano is an excellent example. About a year or so ago she did the math and concluded she could "retire." We're not talking the kind of retirement that would allow her a cottage near the beach either. This would be a very humble retirement. But her decision to leave the work world was driven by a number of very good spiritual indicators: by retiring she could be more involved in the lives of her grandchildren; she could join hobby and special interest groups in our community that would give her greater contact with spiritually searching people; she could be more available for small group Bible study, teaching, and discipleship; and she could volunteer at a local hospital.

Can you tell that Betty hasn't really "retired," but has instead "retooled"? "I'm more satisfied now than I ever was in my career," Betty explained. "We serve a great God and I have the best job in the world!"

All of these, and many more, are options that God may offer for your evaluation. Some of these will be explored in greater detail in the next section. Others have received treatment elsewhere in the book. There are other possibilities which only you will find as you obey Jesus' command to "Go!" So let's go!

Section 2: Case Studies

You're not the first one to attempt this great adventure and I've always found it useful to learn from the experiences of others. Hey, we don't have to learn everything firsthand!

This section includes the stories of seven men and women who have rearranged their lives significantly to follow God. Before we look at their stories however, we begin with the biblical example of Paul.

We know Paul as the great missionary church planter of the First Century. But we can glean helpful ideas from his experience. Let's look at the life of Paul, leather craftsman.

Paul: The Leather Craftsman

Here's a confession: I've secretly wished I could be like the apostle Paul.

He's the guy that most pastors, Bible teachers, and Christian workers look up to—his force of personality, his courage, his endurance, his straight-shootin' forthright style and, the thing I admire the most—his success. Man, could that guy win people to Jesus and get churches going. Sure, he had the occasional stoning, whipping, or shipwreck to deal with, but for the most part Paul would roll into town and get things moving. People were converted, pagans were baptized, and Christian communities were started. And he did this not just in a couple little villages or one specific region, but all over the "world" of his day. You could count on either a riot or a revival.

Several years ago I finally had to admit I was more a combination of Peter and Barnabas, not Paul. This was a good realization for me. I pray I can have even a hundredth of a percent of the impact Peter and Barnabas had. Yet, I've still gained much by considering Paul's life and ministry.

So how does this fit into the idea that God may want to make some change in my life? As I've mentioned in previous chapters, my own questioning along this path was triggered by a number of circumstances and insights. One of those is that I wanted my life to make a difference for God. Specifically, I wanted to plant small communities of believers and train people who could do the same. I became convinced this was the heart of God's plan. And who better to consider than Paul on that topic.

Plus, if you're serious about learning the Bible you can't avoid Paul, since a large part of the New Testament was written by him, at God's command and inspiration. As I've looked more closely at this larger-than-life figure, there are two features directly related to our topic: during a normal week Paul probably spent more time making tents or punching holes in leather than church planting and Paul willingly gave up social stature and career success for the sake of following Jesus.

In Acts 18, Paul's co-worker and perhaps his best friend, Luke, notes that Paul left Athens and went to Corinth, a coastal city in southern Greece. While there he met Aquila who was in town with his wife Priscilla. They all had something in common—they were leather artisans, people who could take animal hides and make them into useful items like tents, belts, pouches, etc.

Paul found these folks and decided to work alongside them. And that's the first thing he did when he got to Corinth. Sure, he started preaching about Jesus in the synagogue that following Saturday, but the first order of business was starting his business.

My mind doesn't gravitate to Paul's vocation as a master craftsman of fine Corinthian leather, but as the great first century leader of the church. But the more I've looked into this, I cannot escape that Paul spent a lot of time building temporary housing structures, i.e. tents. To think of him otherwise is shallow and incomplete. Paul's authority as a servant for Christ partly radiated from his decision to work.

He talks about it in his letters to the Corinthian church: "We work hard with our own hands" (1 Corinthians 4:12a, NIV); "As servants of God we commend ourselves in every way … *in hard work*, sleepless nights and hunger" (2 Corinthians 6:4–5, NIV; emphasis added); "I have labored and toiled and have often gone without sleep" (2 Corinthians 11:27, NIV).

He also talks about it in his letters to the church at Thessalonica:

"Surely you remember, brothers, our toil and hardship; *we worked night and day* in order not to be a burden to anyone while we preached the gospel of God to you (1 Thessalonians 2:9, NIV; emphasis added). He repeats this later, "We worked night and day, laboring and toiling so that we would not be a burden to any of you (2 Thessalonians 3:8b, NIV).

And he highlights his difficult money-making toil to the leaders of the church in Ephesus, as recorded in Acts 20, "You yourselves know that these hands of mine have supplied my own needs and the needs of my companions" (Acts 20:34, NIV).

This last statement may be the most remarkable since we know Paul taught every day in Ephesus for two years (Acts 19:9–10). So he was stitching, shaping, and fashioning durable personal goods for part of the day, teaching and proclaiming the Gospel the other half. No wonder he often went without sleep.

I've never worked with leather. There must have been a certain kind of creativity Paul got to explore. I enjoy seeing a written work completed. There's a satisfaction from transferring vague notions into concrete ideas using the right combination of words.

Did Paul know any of that as a shaper and stitcher of tanned animal skin? I wonder about that. I assume he felt some deep satisfaction as an author of Scripture. Who could write 1 Corinthians 13 and not be moved? But when you consider leather crafting, you get the impression Paul saw his profession as no more than a job, a way for him to earn his keep while doing the really important thing God wanted him to do—helping people understand and believe in Jesus and starting up churches.

Paul had his following and yes, many non-Christian people understood his main purpose had nothing to do with tent making. But in his own day, Paul didn't possess the social stature related to career achievement that we so admire. And to be sure, his real 'career,' as we define it, was leather craftsman or tent maker.

Paul hardly made any money doing the thing he's known through history for—spreading the message about Jesus to non-Jews and helping the fledgling Christian church off the ground. Telling people about Jesus was Paul's vocation—the work God designed and destined him to do.

For me, the justifications begin:

"But Paul didn't have a family to support." Paul apparently didn't have a wife (1 Cor. 7:7) and he never mentions children. Although I find his statement in

Acts 20 interesting, "These hands of mine have supplied my own needs *and the needs of my companions*" (Acts 20:34, NIV; emphasis added). Apparently Paul was taking care of his Christian co-workers in addition to himself.

He supported his "family" as he knew it, the other guys who went with him to start churches. But still, no braces to buy, no doctor bills (Dr. Luke went along on almost every trip—sweet!), and no credit card debt.

"But Paul didn't own a home or have a mortgage to pay." Yes, very true. And for many touched by his ministry, home ownership was a given. They weren't going to travel like Paul, and he understood that.

But I wonder, if Paul had been forced to locate somewhere for awhile, say ten years or longer, what kind of home would he have shopped for? I think his statement in Philippians 4:12b is helpful, "I have learned the secret of being content in any and every situation, whether well fed or hungry, whether living in plenty or in want" (NIV).

I imagine Paul would have found a home that allowed him to follow God, probably a modest dwelling suitable for having folks over and studying the Bible. I doubt he would have trapped himself in a distracting debt situation.

No overtime for Paul just to pay off the in-ground pool or the addition in the back, unless he believed God wanted to use the pool or the extra bedroom for some grander goal. But I don't think he would have ventured into such a time-consuming financial strain without a lot of prayer to make sure it fit with the Great Commission.

But we must admit, in the final tally, Paul didn't

have a mortgage to contend with. I have one and you do too, or you likely will someday.

"But I'm no Paul." That's for sure. And I'm not sure any of us are meant to be. Even some of the missionaries Julia and I know are not like Paul in what they've suffered, and some of them have gone through plenty. Paul endured an incredible, almost surreal level, of deprivation physically, socially and emotionally. He's hard to relate to in one sense, although his devotion and passion are inspiring. He was sold out to the highest degree, to the point of being beheaded at the hands of the Romans, according to church tradition.

But I think if I'd known Paul face to face, I might have seen a very different man. I would see a humble, down-to-earth fellow, who didn't like to talk about his painful hardships. He gained no sense of self-righteous satisfaction from out-dueling other Christians in the degree and intensity of the problems he faced for the Gospel. Defending his ministry drove him to discuss these things (2 Corinthians 12:11).

So how do I take Paul's command in 1 Corinthians 11:1, "Follow my example, as I follow the example of Christ" (NIV)? Context helps. This comes on the heels of Paul's observation that he tried to "please everybody in every way," not living out his freedom in Christ at the expense of someone else's conscience. His main point is in 1 Corinthians 10:33, "For I am not seeking my own good but the good of many, so that they may be saved" (NIV).

Then Paul says, "Follow my example."

Here's the measuring stick. Does my work—whether a domestic engineer, part-timer at the fabric store, lathe operator, lawyer—whatever it is, permit me to "seek the good of many, so that they may be saved"?

Paul's work as a tentmaker allowed him to "seek the good of many." But how so?

Being a tentmaker kept him from being a financial burden on new churches. He mentions this to the Thessalonians when he notes that "as apostles of Christ we could have been a burden to you, but we were gentle among you, like a mother caring for her little children" (1 Thessalonians 2:6b-7, NIV). Paul made money as a tentmaker so the Thessalonians would have a better opportunity to hear and act on the Gospel.

Being able to do this was personally satisfying for Paul. The Corinthian church had wrongly concluded Paul was a subpar apostle because he hadn't demanded compensation. He clearly states he has a right to payment but affirms, again, that he made due by the sweat of his own brow (1 Corinthians 9:6).

Since monetary gain wasn't a motivation, what was? "Just this: that in preaching the gospel I may offer it free of charge, and so not make use of my rights in preaching it" (1 Corinthians 9:18, NIV).

For Paul there was a certain spiritual energy generated by his decision *not* to get paid. He knew he had a right to monetary reward but declined that because of the benefit produced in his ministry. Perhaps the Holy Spirit used this choice to keep Paul centered on the main thing: broadcasting the news about Jesus. We know from Romans 7 he had problems with coveting. Maybe having too much money would have tripped Paul up. Perhaps the refusal of income hiked up his Spirit-dependence and infused his ministry with more oomph.

Being a tentmaker allowed him to set an example of hard work for new Christians. Paul knew that his ministry was not confined to telling, but also showing. So he mentions in 2 Thessalonians 3 that his daytime job backed up his instruction, "For even when we were with you, we gave you this rule: 'If a man will not work, he shall not eat'" (2 Thessalonians 3:10, NIV).

This example also gave Paul greater authority for addressing a problem in that church:

> We hear that some among you are idle. They are not busy; they are busybodies. Such people we command and urge in the Lord Jesus Christ to settle down and earn the bread they eat.
>
> 2 THESSALONIANS 3:11–12 (NIV)

How can I set an example of hard work without being consumed by work or volunteerism? In our society "self" is the main reason for working hard or volunteering. How much money do I get? How many perks do I receive? What kind of positive strokes will I earn? That mindset is tempered by the next truth.

Being a tentmaker allowed Paul to show one of the main reasons for having a job—supplying the needs of other people. He comments on this to the Ephesian church leaders in Acts 20. His last statement to them was this:

> In everything I did, I showed you that by this kind of hard work we must help the weak, remembering the words the Lord Jesus himself said: "It is more blessed to give than to receive.
>
> ACTS 20:35 (NIV)

He affirms this notion in his letter to the same church: "He who has been stealing must steal no longer, but must work, doing something useful with his own hands, that he may have something to share with those in need" (Ephesians 4:28, NIV).

Here's a radical idea. One of the main reasons for working should be other-centered kindness. Without question, I need to buy food, clothing and shelter for myself and family. That's biblical (1 Timothy 5:8). There are some who need to ponder that idea more closely.

But it doesn't stop with those who I'm related to by blood. I should work so I can help others out—the person in need, the stranger, the Christians or non-Christians around me whom God wants me to lend a hand. In so doing, I follow the example of Jesus with my money (2 Corinthians 9:13).

Charity was one of the most stunning features of the early church:

> Selling their possessions and goods, they gave to anyone as he had need. Every day they continued to meet together in the temple courts. They broke bread in their homes and ate together with glad and sincere hearts, praising God and enjoying the favor of all the people. And the Lord added to their number daily those who were being saved.
>
> ACTS 2:45–47 (NIV)

Smack dab in the middle of all the signs and miracles was the sacrificial lifestyle of the first Christians. Speaking of this, Martin Robinson and Dwight Smith note, "They won the favour of the people, not just by virtue of their wonder-working miracles, but more by their honest compassion."[1]

Sadly, this trend has diminished in the American church. Even though born-again Christians were three times more likely than all U.S. adults to make a giving commitment (or tithe) to their local church, this still represented a measly nine percent of this category in 2004. Born-again believers donated about $1400 a year per household in 2003. "When contributions are examined as a percentage of household income, giving to religious centers [within the total U.S. population] represents about two point two percent of gross income," the Barna Group web site reported.[2]

But did Paul use his tent making endeavor for ministry? Is that a reason for working? There are Christian ministries committed to helping men and women see their workplace as a mission field, as a place where God wants to use them to live and speak for Jesus.

Paul never speaks of doing this, though you'd have to think he did, especially as you consider his comments to the Colossians:

> Be wise in the way you act toward outsiders; make
> the most of *every opportunity*. Let your conversation
> be always full of grace, seasoned with salt, so that
> you may know how to answer everyone.
> Colossians 4:5–6 (niv, emphasis added)

Or consider his self-description in 1 Corinthians 9:22: "I have become all things to all men so that by all possible means I might save some" (niv). Would Paul have answered a spiritual question, even as he sweated and struggled at his job, dealing with back and joint pain in a world without anti-inflammatory drugs? I think he probably would have.

. . . .

Paul: The Privileged Child

. . . .

As a tentmaker, Paul would have been part of the middle class. But that's not how life started for him. Check out his resume:

> I am a Jew, born in Tarsus of Cilicia, but brought up in this city. Under Gamaliel I was thoroughly trained in the law of our fathers and was just as zealous for God as any of you are today. I persecuted the followers of this Way to their death, arresting both men and women and throwing them into prison, as also the high priest and all the Council can testify. I even obtained letters from them to their brothers in Damascus, and went there to bring these people as prisoners to Jerusalem to be punished.
>
> Acts 22:3–5 (NIV)

Gamaliel was one of the best known rabbis of Paul's day. Bible scholars speculate Paul's family must have been a family of means to send him halfway around the Mediterranean for Scripture training.

In addition, we also know Paul was a Roman citizen, a privilege not conferred on everyone. Bible historians have suggested Paul's family may have done a favor for the Roman Empire and citizenship was conferred on the whole family, in perpetuity.

In addition to a family background which would have aided his career pursuits, Paul was no slacker; he was a go-getter. He says of himself in Philippians 3, "In regard to the law, a Pharisee; as for zeal, persecuting the church; as for legalistic righteousness, faultless" (Philippians 3:5b-6, NIV).

Paul was among the 600 men who qualified for inclusion in one of the most exclusive religious clubs ever—the Pharisees. His zeal for Judaism was unquestioned—he was a persecutor of the church. His commitment to the legal code of the Pharisees was unblemished. Paul was a man who could hold his head up and look down on anyone.

Paul was an up-and-comer, a rocket ship with a breathtaking arc of trajectory. As he tells the Galatian Christians, "I was advancing in Judaism beyond many Jews of my own age and was extremely zealous for the traditions of my fathers" (Galatians 1:14, NIV). Any father would have been proud to have Paul for a son-in-law: upstanding family, strong commitment to church tradition, and a career fast-tracker.

But as we know, Paul ditched all that for the sake of another call in his life. He is transformed, in the eyes of his peers, from one of Judea's most eligible bachelors into a traitor at worst, a noteworthy underachiever at best.

Here was a young rabbi with more potential in his big toe than many possessed in their whole selves. He had so much potential, but spent most of his life exhausting that early personal advantage working for the cause of a mostly problematic Jewish cult called "Christianity." To some who knew him early on Paul was likely a cautionary tale, not the great history-maker we know.

Paul explains his dramatic change of course in the Philippian letter:

But whatever was to my profit I now consider loss for the sake of Christ. What is more, I consider everything a loss compared to the surpassing greatness of knowing Christ Jesus my Lord, for whose sake I have lost all things. I consider them rubbish, that I may gain Christ and be found in him, not having a righteousness of my own that comes from the law, but that which is through faith in Christ—the righteousness that comes from God and is by faith. I want to know Christ and the power of his resurrection and the fellowship of sharing in his sufferings, becoming like him in his death, and so, somehow, to attain to the resurrection from the dead.

Philippians 3:7–11 (niv)

In considering these words, we must first acknowledge that Paul is speaking of his mindset before Christ—obtaining a right standing with God through obedience to the law. This had been Paul's all-consuming passion.

What is my passion? Why do I expend so much energy doing what I do? Do I believe I'm making an impact beyond my lifetime? Am I striving for the approval of peers or parents? Am I shooting for a title or award that will somehow validate me? My goal has never been religious righteousness, but the way I choose to spend my time, whether in a career, raising a family, helping others, or whatever I may choose to do, means something to me within an overall life philosophy. So as I read Paul's comments, I should keep this in mind:

What was to my profit I now consider loss for the sake of Christ. Everything about Paul's life would have been viewed positively in Jewish society, especially his pursuit of manmade righteousness. Paul was a golden child, an exceptional convergence of talent and opportunity that he tossed away like a used tissue.

Why? For the sake of Christ. In fact he considered everything a loss compared to "the surpassing great-

85

ness of knowing Christ Jesus my Lord." In other words, anything previously related to achieving his life goal of God's acceptance based on religious zeal was now viewed as squandered effort. The word so nicely translated "rubbish" in modern English comes from a word which mainly would have meant animal excrement in Paul's day—he considered achievement from his previous life as cow or horse manure. Any time spent pursuing God's approval via religious "perfection" was a true waste of time because it kept Paul from God's acceptance through Jesus.

Now, was Paul's rabbi training garbage? Well, no, of course not. Paul's training in religious argumentation shows up in his letters, and, with the empowerment of the Holy Spirit, this same training was used to baffle enemies and win converts (Acts 9:19–22). He could detect Old Testament scripture twisting and confound the twisters.

Did Paul's understanding of Greek philosophy have no value? Certainly it did. He used his knowledge of Greek poetry before the Athens' city council (Acts 17:28).

Did his whole experience as a Jew, prior to meeting Jesus, mean nothing at all? Paul's observation in 1 Corinthians 9:20 should confirm the value of his former life: "To the Jews I became like a Jew, to win the Jews" (NIV). Jews would listen to him because he knew and followed Jewish custom and tradition.

No, Paul is not saying his whole existence before Jesus was worthless. What was worthless was his hope in these outward facets of life. But God took all this past life and made it valuable in his grander scheme.

I don't always see everything "as a loss" compared to knowing Christ. I've loved my vocational path. I've loved, at times, what my line of work told me about myself—you're talented, you do something unique, you get to use your mind to make money, other people know you because of your work, you do something important in the eyes of others.

My friend Mark went through a job change recently. As he began looking for new work he faced many doubts—I'm too old, I don't have anything to offer, I need more education. These thoughts bore down on Mark like hammer strikes on a nail. But God used these negative assessments, none of which was true, to bring Mark back to square one. "God stripped away all the other ways I've seen myself as valuable and brought me back to the truth that I'm his son through Christ and he loves me," he told me.

From there, the Lord reminded Mark of his faithfulness during the ups and downs of his work life. God jogged Mark's memory regarding his track record of provision. Mark used that recollection as a witnessing platform with anxious and upset co-workers who also faced job loss. Mark did find another job, by the way, where God is using him in the lives of new and old friends.

I want to know Christ. Paul had "known" Christ for probably thirty years by the time he penned these words. Didn't he know Jesus yet? Paul knew there's no end to "knowing" Christ—the infinite, gracious author of life. And Paul wanted to know Christ even better. Just as in a great marriage, where both spouses continue to make discoveries about one another, Paul knew there was so much more to know about Jesus. Paul explains in the next part:

The power of his resurrection and the fellowship of

sharing in his sufferings, becoming like him in his death, and so, somehow, to attain to the resurrection from the dead.

PHILIPPIANS 3:10 (NIV)

Paul describes the process of trusting Christ in the middle of circumstances where his own self-effort was put to death. Paul's trust in himself and his own power was laid to rest as he tried to follow God. Instead, as Paul followed the Holy Spirit's promptings and God's truth in the face of his weakness and fear, the Lord poured his power into Paul, the same power that raised Jesus from the dead.

God raised Paul to new life, giving him vigor and perspective to carry on for Christ in totally improbable situations—to love those who hated him, to care for those who didn't care back, to sacrifice for those who were selfish, and to risk his life for the sake of sharing this news about Jesus. As Dennis McCallum notes, this was the meaning of Paul's reference to the "resurrection from the dead" in Philippians 3. Paul was not referring to his ultimate resurrection, but was describing a quality of life he sought in his everyday earthly existence.[3]

What Paul relates is a life of adventure, power, and purpose that everyone dreams of. But it was only possible as he sought after Christ with abandonment, counting everything as loss, except his relationship with Jesus.

Sounds great doesn't it? But I find in me a desire for what's comfortable, what's predictable, and what I've counted on in the past for an ego buzz. Sometimes that has to do with being a writer. I've worked long enough as a freelancer now that I can Google my name and run across listings of articles I've written over the years, including the first story I ever sold.

There have been times when I've turned to career as a salve for ministry or personal failure. I may stink as a Bible teacher but I can still earn a paycheck reporting on criminals for the local newspaper. I may have some major selfishness problems but everyone at the writers' conference thinks I'm a swell fellow. Maybe this young guy I've been meeting with just told me I'm a lousy mentor, but Fred the magazine editor still wants my stories.

At other points I've retreated into my identity as a dad and husband. Rather than face some character issue or deal with the fallout from a home Bible study setback, I've chosen to circle the wagons. Just me and the family. Not that anyone would have been able to pick that up. I was still connecting with other people outside the family, but not as much and not as deeply. It was a gradual pulling away, an inch or so at a time—a few less phone calls, a few less nights out with friends, a few less penetrating questions for brothers in Christ or revealing statements about my relationship with God. But I felt good about being a spouse and dad.

Entering into the fullness of "knowing Christ" will mean walking with God through the difficulty of such times, without trying to escape emotionally and mentally into my identity as someone else. Instead of retreating into career or being the best daddy or the homeroom parent, I need to keep meeting with other Christians who will ask the hard questions; keep asking God to search me and change me; keep looking into the Bible to gain a sense of who I am and what's really important; and keep loving and caring for people in my sphere of influence.

And hopefully, as I choose this response more rather than less, I'll have a measure of that same result Paul sought, of helping others cross the line from judged to forgiven.

Phil Wong: Following the Past into the Present

Phil Wong graduated from the University of Michigan in 1989 with a bachelor's degree in mechanical engineering, then earned a master's in bio-engineering from the University of California in San Diego in 1991. He has worked for Ford, 3M Healthcare, and Terumo Cardiovascular Systems, an Ann Arbor, Michigan based company that designs and manufactures products used during cardiac surgery.

Phil went to work for himself beginning in the summer of 2005. His reason: he wanted to leverage the profits from his engineering consulting business to address a problem a world away—the horrible situation for baby girls in China.

"After I finished my master's, Kristin and I decided to teach English as a second language in China," Phil explained. "It was a very cool year reaching out to people and sharing the Gospel. We thought about staying there long-term but instead returned to the United States in summer 1992."

Upon his return from China, Phil became a full-time job hunter, even though the experience left a permanent mark on his heart. He spent a difficult nine months looking for that first job and found his opportunity with Ford, who hired him as a test engineer. "I learned good things there—how a big company works, the political life of a big company, how executives make decisions," Phil related. "But I got to a point where I wasn't learning very much and it was wearing me down."

Phil switched to 3M Healthcare, a division of the 3M company. "It was a great break for me," he said. "They were looking for engineers to work on a new heart-lung machine for use during heart bypass surgery. I learned a lot about engineering, design, how to use a CAD (computer aided design) system—all great stuff."

• • • •

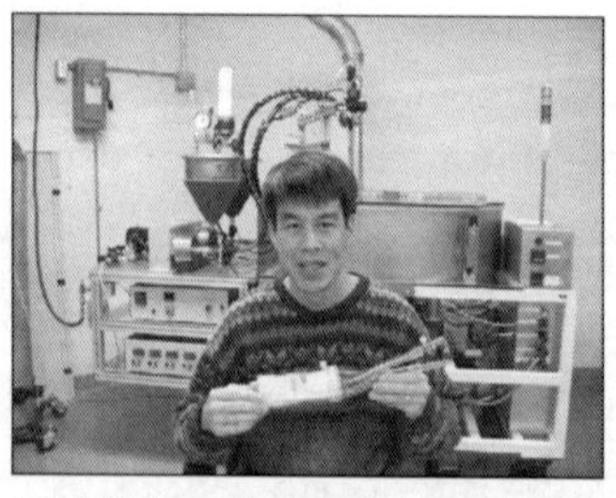

"I think about those girls in China … and there's a resonance in my soul. I've got to help them."

Phil Wong holds a ventilator he developed for use during open heart surgery. He's using money from his engineering consulting business to fund a book about Chinese adoption.

• • • •

But even as exciting as it was for Phil to grow as an engineer, and work in the field in which he'd studied, he felt restless. "I thought about going on staff with InterVarsity (Christian Fellowship) and wrestled with that decision," he said. "Then I went to a homeschooling conference and learned that a high percentage of homeschoolers had gone into business for themselves. I got really fired up about that idea."

Having a home business would allow Phil to connect more with his wife Kristin and his kids, Kathryn, Clara, Benjamin, and Josiah, all of whom are home schooled. "I felt like it was a chance to go back to those days before the industrial revolution, when families would farm together, rather than dads working away from home and not see the kids that much," Phil offered.

So Phil went to work for himself. Since then he has worked on a ventilator that pumps liquid with a high capacity for carrying oxygen. "That was a great project to work on," he said. "The device has been tried on sheep but is not approved for human use. Because I was able to complete the prototype on a faster time frame—it was finished in six months—the learning cycle was exciting."

He's also written and published a book that takes him back to China. "A bachelor there adopts an abandoned baby girl, raises her and experiences the joys and trials of fatherhood," Phil said. "But as he gets older, he realizes he can't take care of his daughter forever, so he arranges a marriage for her. Even though it's painful for him, he gives away the bride and experiences a deep time of loneliness. However, in the end he is rewarded with a granddaughter."

Through the book he touches on another area of

personal passion—adoption. Kristin and he adopted Benjamin and Josiah, both from Vietnam. Kristin wrote about the experience in a book published in 2005, *Carried Safely Home: The Spiritual Legacy of an Adoptive Family.*

The first edition of Phil's book is in English. People who've adopted from China and those considering Chinese adoption are the initial target audience. He's hoping to generate enough capital to launch a second edition in Chinese, which would focus its marketing toward Mainland China.

"I hope to change the minds of people there about daughters, who are often aborted or abandoned because of China's one-child policy and the preference for sons," he said. "There's a huge gender imbalance in China. All sorts of horrible things are happening, like teens being abducted and forced to marry. Some have speculated the increased crime rate in China is due to all the single men running around."

Phil is realistic but also hopeful that his book can help reverse a potentially disastrous cultural trend. "I'm just hoping that if God blesses this, that in a couple generations that gender imbalance will be equalized," he said. "That's a dream that energizes me. I've never been so fired up about a work project in my life."

For Phil, his current work situation, where's he combining a love of engineering with his concern for young girls in China is absolutely a God-directed matter. And if you think about it, who in their career plan says, "I think I want to build heart-lung machines and publish books for China." Only an extraordinarily gifted guidance counselor could imagine a scheme to reach those twin goals.

But God delights in blowing apart our often safe

and staid way of thinking about life to fill us with unexpected joy. "He is able to do more than all we ask or imagine, according to his power which is at work within us," Paul writes in Ephesians 3:20 (NIV).

"I feel like all the events of my life are coming together," Phil offered. "Racism was a big problem when I grew up. I lived in an all-white neighborhood and I used to get in a lot of fights. But the Lord was kind to me. He brought me through that and brought healing into my life to help me understand the problem with people, which is sin.

"As I look back at that awful experience, I can see how good came out of it in what God wants me to do. I root for the underdog. Whenever I see someone on the bottom of the heap I identify with them because I know what it's like. I think about those girls in China who are aborted or abandoned and there's a resonance in my soul. I've got to help them; it's not right.

"It reminds me of Joseph. What others intended for evil, God intended for good. It took a long time for me to figure out, but here I am on the other side of it."

God's best for Phil's life does come with a price tag. Phil acknowledges that in his first year he had to draw from savings to keep the family in groceries and pay the mortgage. "The way I tried to set up the business, I took my base salary from my previous employer, adjusted it for additional self-employment tax I'd have to pay, adjusted for health insurance I'd have to cover, then converted that into an hourly rate," he said. "I benchmarked against other designers and came in a little low so I'd be an attractive person to hire."

There have been times when things were a bit thin. "The cash flow has been negative, which is uncomfortable, but I feel like I'm where God wants me to be,"

Phil said. "We're just working hard and hoping he'll provide through the business plan we have in place."

In addition to the financial strain, Phil also knows that his dream of publishing books for China will have to withstand prospective challenges. "Censorship is common practice; copyright law is often violated," Phil admitted. "I don't know what the future has in store."

Then there's the personal side. "I've made some tradeoffs," Phil shared. "I didn't get the Ph.D. and there are people doing more advanced work than I am and sometimes it bugs me. It's hardest when I'm in the grind of cranking out some work and I'll think, *If I was a really great engineer I'd be doing something more interesting and I'd hire someone else to do this for me.* But then I look at the blessings from being at home—watching my kids grow up, being a part of their lives—and doing ministries at church and I think to myself, 'It's all worth it.' That helps me come back to my sane mind. But sometimes it's a struggle to stay sane."

Donna Jordan-Mitchell: A Better Epitaph

Donna Jordan-Mitchell worked thirty years in television news, twenty-two years as anchor at two different stations in Dayton, OH: WDTN Channel 2 and WHIO Channel 7. At Channel 7, she anchored the five-thirty, ten, and eleven o'clock newscasts.

Here was a typical day: She got home by twelve-thirty a.m., slept until just after dawn, exercised for an hour, then worked until three p.m. for her self-started charity, the Launch Foundation. Then it was back to the newsroom till after midnight.

"I had plenty of power, fame, and money, but little or no personal time to enjoy life," she explained.

Donna had earned regional EMMY awards as a television news anchor and for newswriting; served as a Dayton Peace Accord Partner helping forge economic and humanitarian connections between the United States and Bosnia; won trophies for ski racing, golf, tennis, and racquetball. But if the accolades had propelled her, it was the epitaph that stopped her.

"I started thinking about what I wanted carved into my tombstone," she said. "The epitaph might read 'Donna Jordan, EMMY winning anchorwoman who did some nice things' or 'Donna Jordan, a person who worked hard and made a positive difference in other people's lives.' I chose the latter.

"TV has been very good to me," she added. "I've loved every minute of it. Throughout the years I've had an embarrassment of riches in many ways. But now, at fifty-seven years old, I'm eager to give back."

. . . .

"The nation is my mission field and I can touch more people more deeply now."

Donna Jordan-Mitchell left a high-powered career in TV journalism to head up her self-started charity, the Launch Foundation. Launch teaches abused and incarcerated women how to make decisions to improve their lives and the lives of their children.

. . . .

That's when Donna made what some might say is a crazy choice. She retired from her high-paying, high-prestige, high-pressure job in TV news to pursue her newfound and Spirit-led passion—guiding disadvantaged women to a safe and better life.

The Launch Foundation (www.launchfoundation.org) teaches abused or incarcerated women how to make decisions to improve their lives and the lives of their children.

"After receiving emergency help, disadvantaged women return home and face the same stress and dangers that put them in danger in the first place," Donna related. "Or, if the danger is alleviated, they will make bad decisions because they're looking for security. They'll bring a man into their home; the guy ends up shaking the baby, killing it or maiming it for life. It's all based on bad decision making."

The Launch Foundation provides these women with another crucial layer of support to withstand troubles and handle any obstacles to their future success.

Donna found that women being released from prison also need this kind of input. "The state prison system nationwide reports an eighty percent recidivism rate among women inmates," Donna said. "That means eighty percent of them end up behind bars a second time! And they aren't murderers. They end up driving the getaway car or stealing money to buy drugs. And they have two or three children to support once they return home. Clearly, more rehabilitation for women is needed in our prisons."

Launch's eight-week "Women in Transition" workshop is offered free of charge to shelters, agencies, and prisons who serve these women. As the Launch web site explains, the program's goal is "to help women gain greater independence, self-reliance, and make strong, empowering decisions to break the cycle of codependency that can so easily spin their world into a danger-ous place."[4]

A domestic violence victim inspired Donna. Hilda Spurlock lost half her face after being shot by her husband. Donna interviewed her for a TV report but soon realized Hilda's odyssey was more than another one-off feature piece on the evening news.

"Long after Hilda's story aired on television, I found I couldn't stop thinking about her bravery, compassion, and determination to make a better life for herself. She is a hero to me and is a positive role model for any woman."

Donna founded Launch while still in the TV news business. In addition to the demanding schedule of running a national charity and working full time, she also found herself in a predicament when it came to raising funds.

"There was definitely a conflict of interest," Donna said. "Imagine a donor giving me a sizable gift and then having to do a negative story on him the next week. Or someone trying to keep a story from airing by giving the charity a donation. That was a can of worms I didn't want to open.

"I soon realized that my avocation must become my vocation so I decided to quit."

As she left broadcast journalism and immersed herself in the charity, God gave her many, many green lights. "Things were getting more and more difficult in the TV news business," she said. "But once I made the decision to move toward the charity, obstacles started lifting. It was like a neon sign saying, 'Go this way.'"

She remembered meeting with the head of a funding organization for nonprofit groups. She just wanted a little advice but instead the director handed her a pile of paperwork. "I think it's time you started that non-profit you've been thinking of," he said. "Here's how to go about it."

"One thing after another like that kept happening," Donna said. "The Lord kept putting all these people in my path; they were coming to me, not me finding them. It was amazingly easy!"

Another confirmation came through her attorney who helped set up the charity. "I was holding my breath when I got the bill for his services," she said. "I opened it and was astonished. He had diminished the charges to a minimal amount because he said he believed in me and my dream. What a gift!"

This latest phase in Donna's spiritual ascent really began in 1994, when she met her husband Steve.

"I was always on the move in broadcasting," she said. "I never lost faith but I got separated from God a bit. I wasn't talking to him every day."

When she met Steve she was awestruck by his faith and obedience to the Lord. "He's such a wonderful, wonderful believer," Donna offered. "He helped me see how far I'd moved away; I really hadn't fully allowed God to take control of my life.

"My husband is a beacon of goodness," she went on. "Nonbelievers may not know what it is about him, but they want the peace and contentment he has, even in the wake of stressful times.

"In the newsroom, I've never been able to achieve that level of peace as Steve does so effortlessly. It's difficult not to get caught up in all the aggravation and stress of meeting one deadline after another."

In addition to altering her career, Steve and Donna also made the decision to move from Ohio to the East Coast. They moved to Wareham, MA, Donna's hometown, partly to care for her mom, Marilyn, whose health had declined since Donna's dad died. "She was struggling more than she had allowed me to see," Donna said. "She was much more ill than I ever realized. She was living for me to get home."

Marilyn perked up initially. "I even got her walking again," Donna said. "But then things began to fall apart and she faltered even more. She was tired of the struggle, and on her eighty-second birthday she stroked."

Marilyn had two brain aneurysms but was lucid until two days before she passed away. "I lost her on January 2, 2008," Donna related. "New Year's Eve she began to bleed internally so we took her to the hospital. Within hours, I knew she was dying. She no longer recognized Steve and me.

"Mom kept mumbling and reaching up to the heavens as if asking God to embrace her in his loving arms. I tried slipping into that embrace, thinking that maybe it was me she was looking for, but it wasn't. She kept reaching beyond me. So we made her as comfortable as possible and she passed within two hours."

As trying and difficult as it is to see parents age, become ill and eventually pass on, Donna is thankful for God's timing. "I wouldn't have traded a minute of my life in the past year that I shared with her," she said. "Even the dirty diapers and spoon feeding her. We mainly laughed, and she maintained a positive attitude.

"The worse things grew, the more mentally tough she became. She finally got so tired of fighting she asked me not to feel sad. She wanted to be with God in a better place."

Marilyn also gave Donna a salve for the upcoming grief. "Before she died Mom told me not to mourn her but to celebrate her. She told me I was an excellent daughter and had nothing to regret. What a wonderful gift she gave me!"

The Lord has used Donna's experience with her mom. "I had a chance meeting with a husband and wife, two strangers in a restaurant," she explained. "The woman had just lost her Mom, and she wasn't coming around. She's in management in a big firm in Boston and about to lose her job. She's still not showing up to work even though it's been months. Her husband loves her but he's at the end of his rope. She's going to a doctor but it's not helping."

Donna talked with the woman and, as she described it, "gave her some tough love." "I told her that her mother would be so disappointed that she's throwing away everything she worked so hard for and jeopardizing her marriage. I told her, although her husband is loving and compassionate, he can only take so much. If she keeps pushing him away, she will be surprised one day when he's no longer there mentally, emotional, or physically."

When the conversation was over, the woman thanked Donna and said her words had helped her more than anything else she'd heard. "Her husband was overwhelmed," she offered.

Besides caring for her mom, Donna had her own health reasons for relocation. As an asthmatic, she'd had a difficult time with allergies in Ohio. "Now I wake every morning with energy to spare instead of dragging myself out of bed." she said.

She's also discovered a new level of spiritual health since switching from a media career to director of a nonprofit charity. "I'm blissfully happy," she said. "I'm not behind a desk anymore. I travel; the nation is my mission field and I can touch more people more deeply now. Life is easier, less stressful, and far more satisfying."

Rather than thinking she was crazy, TV colleagues told Donna they envied her career switch. "They were delighted for me and wished they were in my position," she said. "If you work as a TV journalist properly there's not much energy left for the rest of life. The divorce rate for TV people is astounding. This business eats people alive."

One of the unexpected benefits of her choice is attending church in peace. "As a broadcaster I'd walk in Sunday and people would say, 'What are you doing here? You don't belong here—you're in the media!' Or, even, 'It's about time you came to church; you probably need it!'"

"Nothing upset me more than being attacked by a believer who just assumed I was a non-believer and a 'left-wing radical' because of what I did for a living," she explained.

"The very fact I was in the newsroom served a useful purpose for Christianity. Other reporters would ask for my take on a particular story to get another perspective. The people who attacked me didn't know me personally or understand my belief system. If they had thought about it I'm sure they would have realized we need more Christians in the newsroom, not less."

Other times people would walk up to her during the pastor's message to offer a story idea or to give their opinion about television. "People would step right up and complain about how we handled some story or perhaps even complain about my appearance. And they would do that right in the middle of the sermon.

"I quickly found I couldn't have any privacy with

God even in the house of the Lord," she noted. "I stopped going to church because of that."

Today, Donna's much freer to discuss her faith. "Before, when I spoke to a group, people wanted to hear about television, not God. I couldn't lead people to the Lord on my TV station's nickel. But now I have greater freedom to talk about my relationship with God."

Donna knows her new path will have difficulties. She was crushed when Launch was rejected for a grant for the first time. "Steve told me, 'God is moving you in a new direction; listen and adjust. Just backtrack and you'll soon be heading down the right path again.'"

She regains a correct perspective on such setbacks when she remembers this is about God, not Donna. "I've always moved forward at a rapid pace but now I'm moving toward the light," she said. "I'm learning to let God take control."

Tim Norman: Different Soil, More Fruit

Tim Norman is a soft-spoken guy, a university professor with an engineering background, a fellow who you might expect to play it cautious and go with the flow. But he's gone through some serious rototilling to bear more fruit for God.

Tim served as director of the Musculoskeletal Research Center at West Virginia University from 1996 to 2003, three of those years as interim chief. He headed up research in general orthopedics, looking into questions of how bones break and heal, how the human body responds to artificial implants, and bone mechanics.

But in 2003 he moved, physically and career-wise. He is now professor of mechanical and biomedical engineering at Cedarville University, a Baptist liberal arts and sciences college located 260 miles west of WVU in Cedarville, Ohio.

In making the change Tim went to a job that is a photo negative of his former employment. At WVU, he spent eighty percent of his time doing research and twenty percent teaching one or two classes a year. He teaches two to three courses a semester in his Cedarville post and does research the remainder of his time. He clocks fifty to sixty hours each week, about the same as he did in Morgantown, WV.

But Tim's emphasis is different. At WVU career advancement for himself and wife Robin was foremost. "I was more self-seeking," he said. "My goal was helping other people but I was more into advancing my resume.

"I've changed a lot but part of me has not changed. I'm still interested in doing the best I can and excelling as I did then. But at that time there was more emphasis on 'what am I getting out of it.'"

Several years into his WVU job, Tim read a book on spiritual fruitfulness. "The author was expounding on John 15 and referring to Christ as the vine and how the vine that is not producing will be pruned," Tim related. "That book got me thinking about whether I was spending my time in a way that would honor God."

He became restless. He grew tired of constantly writing grant proposals and looking for new ways to pad his resume. He found himself wondering about the source of satisfaction in his life.

•   •   •   •

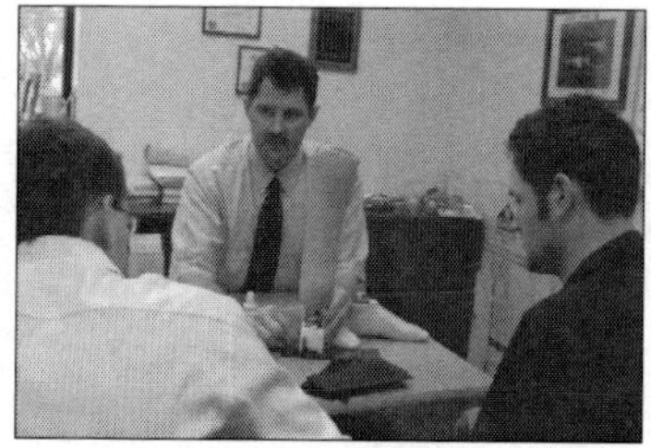

"I wanted to touch the lives of young people in a bigger way."

Tim Norman left a job as director of a biomedical engineering research center at a big East college for a teaching professorship at a Christian university.

•   •   •   •

Although Tim realized God could use him at WVU, he felt a growing dissatisfaction with the university system. "At a state school you do not have the freedom to express your faith," he said. "There's always concern about crossing the line and being brought in for disciplinary action.

"Some might say you'd have more impact at WVU where there's plenty of opportunity for witness and evangelism. You can be effective for Christ anywhere but I didn't feel I was effective there."

Tim began looking for "new soil." "I didn't want to go to another state university," he said. "I wanted to work at a college that stood for something I believed in and where I could aid the mission of that school. I didn't come to Cedarville to be a leading researcher but a great teacher and hopefully continue doing research, just not at the same level and emphasis."

Raised eyebrows, kind rebukes, and questions quickly followed Tim's announcement that he was swapping a high-profile research post for a teaching position at a small, Midwestern Christian university.

"Professors from other universities told me to stay at WVU," he said. "They'd ask me, 'What about your research; where are you going to get labs and grants; you can't do world-class engineering research at a small private school; you need a larger place with lots of facilities.'"

Family members questioned Tim's judgment, although his parents didn't have a conviction either way. "For them I was still continuing as a university professor so they saw the change as a unique opportunity," he said.

Tim sought counsel but even this was hard. "People didn't want to render an opinion," he said, "probably because it was such a life-changing decision and they were fearful of influencing the direction of my life.

"Friends would make comments like, 'That sounds interesting; I don't know what you should do; what do you think?' I'd even get that from clergy not familiar with my path. They'd ask more questions than they answered. Robin and I were pretty much on our own as far as decision making. That was tough."

The costs of leaving have varied. At WVU Tim had the potential of earning almost a third or more than he can now. "But I would have sent my kids to a place like Cedarville for college and now they can attend here at a significantly reduced cost. So I can look at the pay cut, but if I factor in tuition cost the total package is probably close."

Since moving to Cedarville, Robin has established her psychiatric practice. "Before we moved here she was practically a stay-at-home mom," Tim offered. "I took a big pay cut but because she works it helps make up the difference."

With money pretty much a non-factor, the bigger potential item has been prestige. "I'm still able to publish but I don't have the same potential for collaboration," Tim said. "The change to Cedarville has definitely required me to refocus my research and utilize resources I have locally. That's a challenge I've enjoyed.

"However, if you're not in the mainstream there's this perception and potential that you lose your edge. That's been tough to maneuver through." Praying through those negative emotions is Tim's primary defense. "I have to remind myself of my priorities and why I'm doing what I'm doing."

He can also counter those false perceptions with a hard fact: he's having more success in smaller doses than when he was doing research almost exclusively. For instance, Tim was one of only eight presenting on the topic of osteoporosis and biomechanics at the 2007 Orthopedic Research Society meeting in San Diego.

"I'm pursuing newer and fresher ideas than before," Tim said. "And since I'm not driven by the need to bring in dollars or produce papers, I get into discovering things I want to in a more leisurely way and do a better job.

"The only deadline I have is my own. That's been very rewarding and a benefit that flows out of my position here."

While the Cedarville post has provided opportunities to satisfy research inclinations, he's experienced the greatest satisfaction from his involvement with students. "That's the reason I moved—I wanted to touch the lives of young people in a bigger way," he affirmed. "It's been incredibly fulfilling to start the biomedical engineering program at Cedarville and provide learning opportunities for these kids that would only normally be found at bigger schools."

The big spiritual payoff for Tim is the chance to lean on God in a bigger way. "To come here I gave up tenure at WVU and that was a big step of faith," he said. "I left it in God's hands and told him, 'You'll have to take care of this.'"

God gave Tim a verse to think about during his transition, "Be still, and know that I am God" (Psalm 46:10a, NIV). This helped him remember that God controls the future, that he's in charge, whether life is going well or not.

"When you step out and say, 'God, I'm putting my trust in you,' your faith grows in ways it wouldn't otherwise. It's not that you have to quit your job to experience that; there are different ways to do this. But if you stay in the safe place and don't give him a chance to show you he's in charge, you shut down a growth path. That's huge."

Jim Jinkins: From Youth Pastor to Animator

"Tarzan" Jinkins, fearless spiritual looker-arounder, begins whacking through the substantial undergrowth of his own mind. He chops his way through a jumble of "what if" vines, then trips over a "false start" bush, but he keeps moving, ever moving. At last he hacks his way into an open field and encounters The Luminous of Understanding. Hold on everyone ... just a moment. Sorry folks, that was just his wife turning on the bathroom light. Back to our regularly scheduled program.

Jim Jinkins is co-founder of Cartoon Pizza, a New York City-based animation company. He's also been a puppet named Minus, an out-of-money grad student, an Emmy-winning Disney cartoon creator, a real estate salesman, a youth pastor, an art director, and an ad agency freelancer. He's also a husband, dad, son, and silly storyteller.

When he was a kid Jim dreamed of being either a forest ranger or Tarzan. In one sense he's living that childhood fantasy, because discovering God's path for his life has been more like jungle exploration than serene contemplation.

"Some might think, 'Well, if I want to discover the Lord's leading I better stay in my dorm room with the lights off and eat potatoes,'" Jim related. "I have a different approach. This message that God leads and cares for me keeps me pushing and trying things, meeting people and thinking. You never know how things will connect."

And connect they have. Jim started his professional life as a youth pastor at Otter Creek Church of Christ in Nashville. And even though he learned tons there, both what to do and what not to do in ministry, he hadn't quite found his place in the wilderness.

"Being a youth minister was something I could handle," Jim said. "I understood it and there was a church looking for one. It's not because I had this intense passion for it, but it was part of my thrashing through to find my path."

While many would assume that a good Christian guy had found his place as a youth minister, Jim felt he was off mission.

"There was something inside me burning, pushing me along," he said. "I couldn't tell you what it was at the time, although you can call it the hand of God leading me where I was meant to go. I hadn't completely discovered what I was supposed to do."

• • • •

> "You never stop learning or needing to be reminded how God really does work."

Jim Jinkins, a former youth pastor, has uncovered God's plan through children's programming and animation. But he's made his way through some very jungle-like phases of life to arrive there.

• • • •

So he quit. The decision to leave the ministry received mostly good responses, even from church members where he served. "They knew I was a kid fresh out of Lipscomb University trying to figure things out," Jim said. "There was a lot of goodwill."

"I matured in that job," he added. "I had no idea what I was doing; I had no idea how to delegate. Some things turned out successful, like the puppet program, and I tried to remember why. It was disastrous from an organizational sense. But that first job helped me tremendously."

His home church in Richmond, VA had a mildly bittersweet reaction. "They asked me to preach any time I was home on college break," he said. "I wasn't getting heavy-duty overt pressure but they were rooting for me to be a preacher. When I left all that for children's television they never asked me to speak in front of the church for any reason even though I still had things to say. I think what happened is they thought, *Jim's moved on; let's look for other people to grow.*"

Most amazing to Jim were his parents. "They're committed to their spiritual lives. My dad's been an elder at Hermitage Road Church of Christ in Richmond, VA for thirty years. My mom's been a Sunday school teacher. So they were happy when I was working at a church. But once I locked on to children's programming they were very excited that I got to use many of my different talents. Plus they saw how excited I was."

This was a familiar pattern to Jim. "If I wanted to join Boy Scouts or the football team they'd say, 'Okay' and get me where I needed to be," he said. "Then they sent me to college and I chose art for my major. I didn't know what I would do with an art degree. It's amazing they didn't insist on something more specific. I hope I'll be that cool with my kids letting them find their path."

"The Path." This is a recurring theme for Jim—discovering, discerning and sometimes stumbling upon God's course. Sometimes the signs are obvious, while others are barely visible till the heart is humbled enough to perceive them. "Finding 'The Path' has always had this very jungly feeling," Jim commented. "I've always been prayerful and I've always been certain God was leading what was going on, although I don't always do a good job of sensing His direction. Even to this day it continues to be this weird, 'I-don't-know-what's-coming-next' kind of thing."

Sometimes God provides trail guides, if we're willing to follow. For Jim, the earliest pathfinders were an orange-tinted guy with a spitty snicker and his banana-headed friend sporting a unibrow.

"I remember the premier of *Sesame Street* in high school," he noted. "It was so different. You had Bert and Ernie and this puppetry that was hip and funny.

Sesame Street was for everybody—the preschooler, teens and adults—it was a co-viewing experience. That was new. I loved it. I looked at the TV and said, 'That's what I want to do.'"

"In youth ministry I was doing puppets, which was a parallel to cartooning in the ministry. I wanted to be a puppeteer and animator—a person telling stories in a cartoony way. That's what was pushing me. But I had no clue how to get there."

Between ministry and grad school at Ohio State University, Jim did his "obligatory wandering in the wilderness." He worked in real estate with another member of the Otter Creek congregation. "There was nothing further away from what I wanted to do but I needed to make money," he said. "Then I went to grad school."

He attended Ohio State, taking classes in film and animation. "I had a great time in college but I didn't take it as seriously as some kids. But I was paying for grad school myself and learning things I wanted to learn. That was spectacular … until I ran out of money. I was marooned."

Jim still had a job, working as puppeteer for a library children's program, but had no idea where to go from there. Then he had a "chance meeting" with a guy at a Columbus, Ohio fabric store, where he was buying material for puppets. "I overheard him talking about a kids' show called *Pinwheel*," he said. "I asked him if they were looking for people and he said I should come down and interview. So I got a job as a puppeteer and graphic artist. There I was running out of money at grad school and God led me to my career! Things connect in unusual ways."

Little did he realize he had arrived at an important

vocational juncture—the birth of Nickelodeon, the first cable channel devoted to children's programming.

From there the path seemed to clear. He performed as 'Minus' the puppet on Pinwheel. Next he served as graphics director for the Children's Television Workshop's *Square One TV* on PBS. He worked as director and production designer on the HBO special, *Buy Me That! A Kid's Survival Guide to Television Advertising*.

He found himself in New York City, mainly working on live-action children's programs for HBO and Nickelodeon. He also picked up freelance advertising work, creating low-end animation to test commercial ideas. God used a friend at one agency to remind Jim about the full range of his gifting.

"This guy told me, 'With your sense of humor and the way you draw you ought to be doing this,'" Jim recalled. "It wasn't like an 'Aha!' moment but a little heads up that helped me believe I could do something in animation.

"My path had taken me various places, into live action, building props and art direction. How neat that someone reminded me of that dream and put it back in my head."

In 1990, Jim and business partner David Campbell created Jumbo Pictures Inc. and produced the award-winning live action series *Allegra's Window* for Nickelodeon. Next came *Doug*, the result of a doodle by Jim on a not-so-great day, but which David saw as having incredible potential.

"David and I have been business partners for eighteen years and from the very beginning there have been miracles," Jim explained. "I appreciate that now more than ever. The whole act of selling a show to a network is such a million-to-one shot. Selling *Doug* was amazing."

Original episodes of *Doug* aired on Nickelodeon from 1991 to 1994. Then Disney purchased Jumbo in 1996 and aired *Doug* on its "One Saturday Morning" slate from 1996 to September 2000. During its run, *Doug* was nominated for four Daytime Emmy awards. The show's success also led to a feature-length film called *Doug's 1st Movie*.

In addition to *Doug*, Jim created *PB&J Otter* and produced the TV show *101 Dalmatians* for Disney. David and he also developed *JoJo's Circus* and *Stanley* for Disney, *Pinky Dinky Doo* in conjunction with the Sesame Workshop and *Global Thingy*, a regular segment on Sesame Street.

Things went extremely well for Jim and David at Disney, despite the problems involved in creating storylines and artwork to satisfy someone else's vision. But they hit a crossroads in 2001: continue to work with Disney and live off the profits of shows they'd already developed or go out on their own.

For Jim it was one more twist in "The Path." He and David decided to leave Disney and open Cartoon Pizza Inc. Almost immediately they were asked to produce sixty-five episodes of *Stanley*, a very highly-rated program for preschoolers that aired on Playhouse Disney. But starting their own animation shop gave these best friends and brothers in Christ a chance to play with another idea suggested during the Disney days.

"A long time ago a mutual friend of ours from church said we should do a series for kids on the Ten Commandments," David explained. "Our knee-jerk reaction was, 'Let me get this straight, you think we should do a series on "Don't commit adultery" and "Don't commit murder.'" We just sort of said, 'Yeah, okay' but didn't do anything with it. But it was gestating in our brains all those years."

When Jim and David went out on their own, gestation turned into full-blown hatching. "David and I both have kids, and we wondered how to teach the principles behind the Ten Commandments, like keeping a promise, obeying your parents, don't steal. These were amazingly universal principles."

They dusted off a concept from the Disney days as a platform for the Ten Commandments show. *Hoopdogz* features a nine-year-old pup named VJ Bumpus who encounters failure and redemption as he tries to live up to God's moral law. The stories have a flare for creative use of color, winsome characters, and a life lesson based on God's truth. Plus, *Hoopdogz* makes you laugh, grin, or otherwise chuckle.

So far Jim and David have produced four of the ten shows: "God Good, Idols Bad" based on the second commandment; "Stealing's Uncool" on the eighth commandment; "God is #1" from the first commandment and; "A Promise is a Promise" which centers on commandment number seven.

"We wanted to do a faith-based project, and we decided instead of lining our pockets with profits from the other shows we'd invest our own money to make *Hoopdogz*," Jim said. "We took everything we learned from *Doug, 101 Dalmatians* and *JoJo* and decided to do our own thing, to own it and creatively control it."

Jim and David funded the first four episodes but discovered they couldn't make all ten this way. Now there's a distribution company that wants to get the shows into a major retail chain. "This is very much a part of our hopeful future," Jim said. "We don't want to be the guys who produced 'The Four Commandments.' We're really determined to get that project back on its feet. Putting up our own personal money was impractical.

"We understand that it takes time and we're in it for the long haul, so we're not panicked. People have to know about *Hoopdogz*. It will take word of mouth to grow it, which takes time. We don't have any guarantee of making all ten and or that it will be successful. We are truly stepping out on faith."

Of course, Jim and David have options. They could work anywhere in the world of animation and pull down handsome six-figure incomes. "One of the safest things we could do is take on creative executive positions in some large company, making nice salaries in a comfortable place to work," Jim said. "But we've never discussed that— it's not our mission. We've been approached and passed up those opportunities. In one sense it would be easy to do, but emotionally, physically, and spiritually it would be crippling."

On the harder days Jim imagines a different, dreamier kind of existence. "Sometimes I think about what it would be like to shut down the company and operate on a smaller scale, just writing screenplays and books and illustrating, some situation where we'd have time to focus on more personal art and less on business plans and corporate meetings," Jim added. "I fantasize about that."

But he pulls out of the daydream in time to remember why he went to work for himself. "We want to make things for kids and families that are entertaining, exciting and have a strong moral underpinning," Jim said. "The decisions we make we make prayerfully. That's all very much at the center of who we are, the shows we make, how we conduct business and how we work with artists and producers."

They haven't felt the strain of financial worries—yet. "David and I stored up enough during the Disney days that we wouldn't be in a panic situation instantly," Jim said. "We felt we had enough resources to take chances and pursue our dream. But it won't last forever—we'll see what happens."

Jim's wife Lisa has been very supportive of his decision to follow God this way. "Lisa's a spectacular person and a great believer in the Lord," he said. "She's more stable in the water than I am; she's the rock. She's been extremely supportive of me as a writer and artist and always supportive of the mission we've been on. Whether it's a great time or a hard time, she stays focused."

And the kids, well, they just like the fact dad's around to make up goofy stories or horse around in the living room. "I felt like I disappeared for eighteen months at a time when I was at Disney, traveling for the company and working on projects," Jim related. "It took a toll on me and a big toll on the family. I have more time to be with my kids. That's the level they operate at— is dad around and can he play."

Jim sees this current adventure as another twist of faith. "Here I am this full-blown adult who's been through many things," he related. "You'd think by now I'd understand this thing about 'The Path,' about trusting in God and knowing full well that I'm cared for. But we just went through two years of wandering in the wilderness.

"We were on the brink of this collapse then we weathered that storm. Now we have our second season of *Pinky Dinky Doo* and it looks like things are ready to take off again. We were blessed with sixteen years of nonstop 'how are we going to get this done' and experienced an unprecedented amount of success. It was an amazing ride. Then we had two years of famine and things got quiet.

"You'd think by now I'd be peaceful but I have moments of panic. You never stop learning or needing to be reminded how God really does work."

Dean Ridings: Good Works vs. "Good" Money

Dean Ridings is director of communications at The Navigators, an international ministry helping people become disciples and mentors of others. Navigators groups can be found on college campuses and military bases around the world. Headquarters for the seventy-five-year-old ministry is Colorado Springs, CO.

Dean's path to The Navigators has involved plenty of navigating, beginning in college. He had served as editor-in-chief of the newspaper at Cal State Hayward (now Cal State East Bay). He had positioned himself to make an easy transition as reporter at the local newspaper. But then he felt "an ache in my heart," as he described it.

"There was a story that captured my attention then—'Library gets new computers,'" he said. "I didn't even need to read that story; the headline told me all I needed to know. I didn't want to labor on stories where a headline said it all. I wanted to write to make a difference for eternity's sake."

This core idea became the touchstone for Dean's life—writing to make a difference for eternity. He sought guidance from his senior pastor and youth pastor at Redwood Chapel Community Church in Castro Valley, CA. Youth pastor Doug Tegner had attended Moody Bible Institute in downtown Chicago and had a number of friends working in the Christian magazine business. He gave Dean the names of six people to speak with and get further direction.

Three of Tegner's contacts encouraged Dean to get a communications degree from a Christian college. He moved to Chicago and earned a master of arts in communications degree from Wheaton Graduate School in 1986.

After grad school he took a position as staff writer with Prison Fellowship (PF), an international ministry founded by Chuck Colson of Watergate fame. PF introduces inmates to Jesus Christ, helps them grow in their faith and then assists them with the transition to life after imprisonment.

He served at PF two years, worked five years as communications manager for another Christian ministry, International Students, Inc. (ISI), then another six years for Christian Camping International/USA (CCI/USA), now known as the Christian Camping and Conference Association.

During the transition from CCI/USA to The Navigators, Dean faced a soul-searching crossroads. He was offered a job spearheading the new communications department for Chinese Children Adoption International, founded by Joshua and Lily Zhong.

"They're believers and needed someone to pioneer their communications effort. Joshua and Lily have such a heart for these kids, particularly the girls in Chinese orphanages. I believe today that salary would be in the six-figure range, had I become a key member of their leadership team."

With all the normal bills to pay, plus four kids to put through college, Dean and wife Kim could have put money from that salary to good use. "But I didn't feel called to it," he explained.

Okay, hold on a minute! Dean is offered a job at an organization doing good work—helping little Chinese girls find loving, permanent families. The organization is run by a Christian husband and wife. How could he not be called?

"Good is the enemy of the best," Dean said. "I don't want to miss God's best. While I have a fair wage with Navigators, I am more desperately depending on the Lord rather than making things happen myself. The Lord is telling me, 'Follow me in my original vision for you, to change people's lives and help them toward greater holiness through my ability to communicate.'

"I have no doubt that working for other organizations I could make a difference for eternity but I sense the Lord saying, 'Stay here; serve me now in this capacity; be faithful for today and you will always grasp my best.'"

• • • •

"How do I know the will of God? Be a living sacrifice, that's how I can know his will."

Dean Ridings (upper left), director of communications at The Navigators, encircled by family (from top right clockwise): daughters Rebecca, Elizabeth, and Sarah; son, Christopher; and wife, Kim.

• • • •

One particular verse has stuck with Dean throughout his career twists and turns, especially when he was cut loose from ISI. "The verse in my devotion the next day was Ephesians 2:10!" he said. "God was assuring me that I am his workmanship, created to do good works he has prepared me to do. That gave me a sense of being in God's perfect plan even though I was down and out with no job and we'd just had our third child, Sarah."

Encouraged by his devotional reading, Dean made the decision to thank God in advance for how he would work things out. Because of divine forewarning, Dean had distributed his resume prior to getting cut at ISI. By the time he was released he'd been contacted by two other organizations.

Ultimately, the big question is this: how do I determine the will of God for my life? Certainly, for some, working at an adoption agency is God's best. For others, serving as a teacher at an inner city school will be the call. Someone else, the Lord may direct to a volunteer position at a crisis pregnancy center. For Dean the most important Bible passage for sorting this out is Romans 12:1–2:

> Therefore, I urge you, brothers, in view of God's mercy, to offer your bodies as living sacrifices, holy and pleasing to God—this is your spiritual act of worship. Do not conform any longer to the pattern of this world, but be transformed by the renewing of your mind. Then you will be able to test and approve what God's will is—his good, pleasing and perfect will.
>
> ROMANS 12:1–2 (NIV)

"I don't refer to this verse lightly," Dean added. "I'm banking on it. How do I know the will of God? Be a living sacrifice, that's how I can know His will. I pray, 'Lord, here I stand on the altar; lead me again today.' And he responds, 'Be faithful for the day, Dean; serve me well today.'"

In addition to Scripture and prayer, Dean has also vigorously sought the wisdom of Christian mentors and friends. "I try to be connected to a pastor, someone I can go to with help on huge life decisions," he said. "I also have some people in my life who are going to love me no matter what."

When Dean finished grad school he struggled about whether to go with Prison Fellowship or another job. "I called Ron Davis, my best friend from high school," Dean said. "I told him about both jobs and he said, 'It's so clear; your heart is with Prison Fellowship.' Right there the Lord was telling me, 'That's true.'"

Dean is very aware that he has a strong inclination to make the "will of God" happen on his own. "That's what Abraham did with Ishmael—I'll make the promise happen, God just needs a little help," he said. "I must be up to date with God every day because I might take one subtle step off the path and find out in five to ten years that I'm a huge distance away from his best.

"I don't have to pound on the door to make things happen. I just have to ask, seek, and knock. I am exactly where he would have me. And if there's another transition he will guide that too."

Dean has relied on this philosophy in church ministry too. From July to November 2006, he served as associate pastor at a sister congregation of his church, Woodmen Valley Chapel in Colorado Springs, CO. He helped facilitate a men's Bible study, contacted first-time visitors and served as interim director of men's ministry.

"I saw the pastoral ministry as fitting in with God's original intention for me," he said, "to help people grow toward greater godliness through written, verbal, and one-to-one communication."

When that job came to an end, Dean's involvement in ministry didn't stop. "All of this is part of the good works God wants me to do," he noted. "I could call the adoption agency today about a job. But it would take me away from the compelling calling of the Navigators as well as the compelling mission of my local church and the ministry I get to be part of though I'm not paid for it.

"I have to go back to Matthew 6—don't worry about the clothes you'll wear or the food you'll eat but seek first my kingdom."

Lydia Hoyle: Guided by Peace

Lydia Hoyle is a divinity school professor. She's also the daughter of two aging and ailing parents, the wife of a psychology professor, and the mother of two teenage boys and an energetic elementary school-age daughter. Lydia Hoyle could use some peace!

Peace is the very thing Lydia has counted on to help her determine the answer to the question "What does God want me to do?" She described it as "a deep assurance that I'm walking in the way I should go."

"I could make a sheet and put all the positives and negatives down, but somewhere deep within me, beyond those positives and negatives, I already know."

Lydia hasn't always been a divinity school professor. She spent twelve years teaching New Testament and church history at Georgetown College in central Kentucky. Before that she was an elementary school and junior high special education teacher, instructing combination classes of learning disabled, emotionally disturbed, and mentally handicapped students. She also served as a part-time youth pastor.

While special education is clearly a vocation within the will of God, Lydia knew before she ever cleaned her first chalkboard she wouldn't work in that field for long.

"I went to Urbana, Ill. for a student missions conference my senior year in college," she explained. "I attended Appalachian State University in North Carolina, so it was a long journey, and I didn't have any friends going. But I felt very compelled to go."

Lydia went to the conference looking for answers to this big question: "What does God want me to do?" "I went to all the booths and visited all the mission organizations, but I never felt called to missions," she said. "I remember thinking, *I don't know where I'm supposed to be.*"

She took a walk alone across the University of Illinois campus. "This young bearded guy came along beside me," Lydia recalled. "He didn't ask my name but just said, 'So, where are you headed next?'"

"I looked at this guy and blurted out, 'I think I'm going to seminary,'" she said. "I looked around, up, and down and thought, *Where did that come from?* I hadn't thought of that at all. I'd never really considered it an option; it never popped into my head before."

• • • •

> "God cares more about who I am than what I do."

Lydia Hoyle is a wife, mom to three kids, daughter to aging parents, and seminary professor. Sensing God's peace has been a key to wearing many hats successfully.

• • • •

By the time Lydia's mind processed what her mouth had spoken and she regained temporal awareness, her walking companion had left. "This fellow was nowhere to be seen, so it had this otherworldly feel to it," she said. "But from that point I was confident I was supposed to go to seminary. I didn't know why or what particular ministry I was training for; I just knew that's what I needed to do next.

"I filled out the application for seminary, and in the section that asked about my calling I just wrote, 'I feel I'm called to train.' That's not what I'm looking to hear from students now that I'm a seminary professor, but from that moment I was confident that's what I was supposed to do."

Near the end of seminary Lydia began asking that familiar question, "What's next?" She loved to teach but also enjoyed ministering to college students. She interviewed for a campus ministry job at the University of Pennsylvania and was offered the position. She also contemplated an academic career. And then God intervened with another young man, one she knew a little better than the bearded stranger at Urbana.

"This was probably the most difficult time figuring out God's plan for my life," Lydia said. "I was getting ready to graduate from seminary when Rick came to visit. We hadn't dated in five to six years but we'd kept in touch. But when he came to Texas, he asked me to marry him. That helped me narrow down my options!"

But she made her decision prayerfully, not breathlessly. "I deliberated several days after Rick proposed," Lydia recalled. "Then I told him 'yes,' but we agreed not to tell anybody for a day and a half. I wanted to wake up two mornings in a row either with a sense of 'Yes, I'm doing the right thing' or 'Oh my gosh!' He asked me on Saturday; I said yes on Tuesday; and we started telling others on Thursday."

Now engaged, she decided against the job in Pennsylvania and instead applied to a doctoral program in North Carolina, where Rick was heading.

"I had a passion for teaching and a lot of curiosity," Lydia said. "I had several professors who were very influential in my life so I was very aware of how God could use that as a ministry. But it's not like I was six-years-old and thought, 'I'll teach religion someday.' Over time I felt confirmed in this decision, but I was really uncertain initially."

"I rarely know what God wants me to do a year from now or five years from now. I know what I need to know for today, and that's how it's always been."

God refined this day-by-day reliance during her first year of studies. "A doctoral program in religious studies doesn't really encourage faith," she said. "In fact it was anti-Christian in some ways. I was a newlywed. I had just finished seminary and came into an environment where evangelical Christians were laughed at. I questioned what God wanted me to do; I didn't feel a lot of peace."

Lydia weighed her options that first year. "I had a degree in special education and enjoyed teaching," she said. "I had a divinity school degree and could have gone into ministry. But none of those seemed like the right thing. So I kept on the journey and asked God to confirm it or show me a new path. I wanted there to be a different path; I was not having fun."

In determining God's direction, Lydia relied on a maxim she has shared with her students, "Never doubt in darkness what God has shown you in the light."

"Don't stop pursuing your calling when things look bad," she said. "You don't want to make a decision in an emotional moment. It's very difficult to hear the call of God in the midst of crisis. Don't make big decisions when you can't hear beyond the rattling in your brain."

She also counted on God working with her aptitudes and interests. "All I am is part of God's calling," she said. "He won't call me to be a trapeze artist when I don't have great balance. It's not that God won't call us to what's uncomfortable, but God's calling will be consistent with how he's prepared us.

"God will draw me toward those things he wants me to do. Not only will he want me to do them, but I'll want to do them. He will change my will to conform to his own."

She toughed out that first hard year in her doctoral program, leaning on God and husband Rick. "Sometimes I don't know if I'm in the will of God till after I've started down a path, and there's confirmation or not," she said. "God wants us to know which way to go; that's my fundamental belief, so I assume God is directing me, and I need to be listening."

After her doctoral studies, she took a job at Georgetown University in Kentucky. She loved her work but after twelve years the Spirit of God called again. On the telephone. "I had never heard of this particular divinity school, but as I talked to the guy I had such a strong sense that I needed to pursue this," she said. "I called Rick as soon as I hung up the phone and told him, 'This is the craziest thing but these folks have called me about a position, and I have a strong sense I'm supposed to talk further.'

"In academics you don't go around applying for jobs unless they have been advertised," Lydia related. "The idea that Rick and I could both find positions simultaneously in the same area of the country seemed pretty unlikely. Plus this took place in February, when most universities had already advertised for open positions, and it was too late for Rick to apply."

Despite this sense of God's nudging, the chances of Lydia taking the new job seemed low. "I didn't say yes till Rick got word from Duke," Lydia added. "I figured if that's where God wanted us then Rick would have a job. They made a place for him and we came here."

Some of her colleagues assumed Lydia was unhappy or Rick had been offered the Duke job first. "They just couldn't accept that we felt like God was calling us," she said. "I was offered the divinity school position then he was able to work out a spot at Duke, not the other way around."

The move was as much a stepping out in faith for Rick as Lydia. He had tenure and was chair of the psychology department at the University of Kentucky

(UK). He left for an untenured position at Duke, relinquishing complete job security at UK.

Since taking her new assignment, Lydia has faced new challenges, from personal health crises to the demands of a busy teaching and public speaking schedule to the stresses of caring for her mother with Alzheimer's disease. Oh yeah, and being a mom to three kids.

"Summer 2006 to spring 2007 was the most challenging year of my life," she said. "Often times I thought, *This is too much; I don't think I can pull this off.* Then I faced my own health problems. I felt overwhelmed.

"Yet at the same time I determined I was not going to turn away from something that was a calling. I won't make a switch until that's the obvious thing, and I have the peace that's the way I'm supposed to turn."

Lydia's confidence in God's calling helped her stay on course. "I've thought many times I should back up and punt, that I had too much on my plate," she said. "But I never felt I could do that, not till God directed me, and not as a response to stress. A lot of times we have to walk through hard spots before we reach the smoother road that lies ahead."

Job flexibility has helped her fulfill her calling as a wife, mother, and daughter. "When I'm supposed to be teaching, I need to be teaching," she said. "But I have a huge amount of flexibility. I generally work four days a week and one half day, usually from home. I can dash off to my parents, check on them and stay overnight. Or I might volunteer in my daughter's classroom. I have most of the summer free and spend that time with the kids."

Even with an elastic schedule, Lydia's moment-by-moment connection with God has been the key to keeping her gaze steady. "As I'm walking across campus to the library and looking at the trees, I'll marvel at the creativity of God," she said. "Or as I'm talking with someone, I can celebrate the fact I have this friendship. It's waking up in the morning and talking to God before I do anything else.

"The most important things happen in the midst of the day—in the moments of waking up, in the moments of looking out my office window. In those little moments it seems easier to hear God's direction, especially when I'm feeling overwhelmed. I've often sensed God telling me, 'Celebrate this day.'"

She's especially centered herself on this perspective in the middle of difficulties. "Life is short, and I've had so many reminders of that lately," Lydia said. "When life's not so cheery, I try to focus on the goodness of God and the blessings of God."

Pursuing God's total package of family life, ministry, and work has meant sacrifices. "I always knew I was making choices that would not put me at the top of my field in terms of publishing," she said. "There are only so many hours in a day. I could choose to work all summer and publish lots more than I do, but instead I spend most of that time with my family."

Lydia makes the connection between her journey with God and her hopes for her kids. "I don't really care about their professions, but I want them to enjoy life," she said. "I want them to have a meaningful and fulfilling life; I want them to leave the earth a better place than they found it. That's part of what God wants for us, to enjoy this gift he's given us."

For Lydia the question of what God wants her to do has always been preceded by a larger, more important question: who does he want her to be?

"God cares more about who I am than what I do," she related. "So I try to know the answer to the second question in the context of the first. If I'm trying to be the person God wants me to be, it will become more obvious what he wants me to do."

Jeff Gordon: Who Owns My Soul?

Jeff Gordon, a Columbus, Ohio internal medicine doctor, became a Christian in 1982. He quickly got involved in the ministry of his church, which is committed to developing home-based Christian communities carrying out the Great Commission. He graduated from Ohio State University Medical School in 1984 and finished a three year residency in 1988.

Then he signed a contract with a hospital-based cardiology group, making a six-figure income for the first five years of his career. He worked a forty-hour-a-week schedule, all daytime hours, and had four weeks vacation. It was a sweet arrangement for a guy wanting space in his life for spiritual growth, family, and ministry.

But in 1993, the two partners in the practice pressed Jeff for more. They wanted fifty to sixty hours a week rather than the forty he had been working. They also wanted him to sacrifice vacation time.

By that point Jeff was leading a home fellowship group, roughly equivalent to pastoring a small congregation, no minor commitment. He was also serving as elder during a time of struggle: his church, Xenos Christian Fellowship in Columbus, OH, was attempting to build a facility to accommodate over 3000 people attending services; they were also confronting a major dispute that would result in more than a thousand people leaving.

"I remember the two partners getting me in this room and saying I wasn't committed," Jeff recalled. "They pulled out the contract of this guy who was just joining the practice, criticizing how much vacation time I had and saying, 'This guy has nothing like you have; we've got to make this fair.'

"The one partner said about the new guy, 'He's practically sold his soul to this corporation.' I just looked at him, shook my head in disbelief and said, 'My soul's not for sale.' And that was the end of it. I could tell it was over."

• • • • •

> "I've got to think through regularly, *Am I doing the right thing or not?*"

Jeff Gordon is an internal medicine doctor, church elder and home Bible study leader. He's chosen a life centered on biblical priorities, but that doesn't mean it's been easy.

• • • • •

Jeff was extremely disappointed. In addition to the schedule and vacation, he enjoyed the work. He took care of patients in the hospital from the time they had heart surgery till they went home. But this phase in his career was over.

"I felt it was way too important to get away with family for me to give up the vacation time," Jeff offered. "Secondly, and this was the main thing, it would have been impossible for me to do ministry and maintain my roles in the church under the proposed job conditions.

"I believed God had opened certain doors to serve in the church and I didn't feel it was right for me to back out. I wasn't leaving my career for the sake of trying to find something else."

By this point in Jeff's life his career was in God's hands, not his own. "Each step of scaling back it's been God saying, 'Here's an opportunity, which way do you want to go?'" he relayed. "It's not like I said, 'I don't like this so I'm going to dump it and find something else to do.' I get suspicious of that kind of thinking."

Jeff went to work for a new practice, which offered him even more schedule flexibility. The timing was perfect because Jeff agreed to teach Christian theology and practical ministry classes three hours a week at his church. The coursework offered to lay members is accepted by a Columbus-area seminary for master's degree credit.

"With the new job I had time to get away and prepare," he said. "This was an important time for me to develop a more thorough understanding of the Bible and theology."

Jeff made another job change in 1998. He now works one week a month, teaching internal medicine to family practice residents at Grant Hospital in Columbus. He also works for his church.

Jeff started his career looking for employment that would permit him to lead a home-based Christian community and disciple others. "As a professional you are in the position to say, 'This is how I want to live,' and try to find a situation that fits the bigger values you're trying to live by," he said. "It may seem impossible to prioritize around God's values, but he will lead you into a career situation that will work."

From Jeff's perspective, the problem isn't do-ability, it's want-ability. "One of the biggest problems I see is overspending," he said. "I see this in residents who are moonlighting, doing all this stuff because they're in big debt with student loans and spending more than they make. Now they're into a whole life wrapped up in that bad habit and they're always behind, always nervous."

Making choices centered on God's values and priorities has led Jeff to a life of great wealth personally and spiritually, even though his material existence is modest in comparison with other American physicians.

"There's definitely status you give up by not living in the same neighborhoods and driving fancy cars and going out to prestigious places to dinner all the time," Jeff commented. "Guys who graduated with me from med school, who've been out for over twenty years now, are seeing the luster of that lifestyle fading.

"The status of someone who's done something different has gone up and they're saying, 'I wish I could do what you're doing,' but it's taken them twenty years to see it. They thought I was crazy twenty years ago."

Going against cultural expectations has been tough for Jeff. He has to revisit who he is as a child of God, someone loved and treasured and who's been redeemed for the Lord's purposes rather than his own. This outlook and its implications has put him at odds with people he respects and whose opinions he values.

"One of the most memorable lines came from a mentor of mine, someone highly respected at the hospital where I did my residency," Jeff said. "This man told me, 'You really could have made something out of your life' with the implication 'You haven't.'

"This is hard stuff. The world tells you, 'These kinds of people are successful' and it's based on all this superficial, external stuff, yet those messages are so loud and pervasive you can't avoid them. Even today I've got to think through regularly, *Am I doing the right thing or not?*

Fortunately for Jeff he's made these changes with the full support of Laura, his wife. "She wasn't pressing for material advancement and big houses and cars so we were on the same page from the beginning," he said. "Second to your relationship with God, the most important thing is agreeing with your spouse on basic values."

He also has brothers who help keep his head straight. "I need a couple guys in my life who are pursuing God and trying to live a life of faith to remind me it's real and true, not just a theory," Jeff said. "I remember listening to a Howard Hendricks tape years ago and he said every guy needs a Paul, a Barnabas, and a Timothy—someone to look up to, someone who's a peer, and someone you can help grow. I've tried to follow that.

"Each of these relationships reminds you of reality and helps you see yourself more clearly. We need someone who offers us something to strive toward; we need someone who reminds us of the mistakes of spiritual youth; and we've got to have someone who's at the same level and is committed to the same end."

More than anything, Jeff continues to forge an intimate trust in Jesus. "You have to get in there with him daily through Scripture, prayer, meditation, journaling," he said. "All those things root who you are in him, otherwise it just slips away. The cultural consensus holds too much power."

Jeff has discovered many tremendous side benefits from his decision to give God his medical career. "When it comes to communicating values to your family what you say is small in comparison to what you do," he offered. "You can tell your kids it's good to follow God, but if they don't see it in your life, it's a dead letter.

"Because of the way we've prioritized our lives, going to fellowship or having their own commitment to home group has never been questioned. This is the way we live. We've had a high school boys Bible study group every Friday for fifteen years; we've had home church meetings in our house; people from out of town stay with us. Our kids have seen how we lived what we believed and served other people. They've just grown up with it."

Jeff and Laura's kids have also seen and done amazing things because of their dad and mom's choices. They've visited missionaries in Southeast Asia; their youngest daughter visited India; their son and some other kids built a house in Mexico.

"We've canoed in Canada; we worked with Habitat for Humanity in South Dakota. They've just gotten to be in the mix of things. When we've taken high school students on retreats, our son was with us, even when he was eight or nine."

Jeff has also seen another interesting fallout from putting Christ first—he's a better physician! "I'm in medical education and it's amazing to me how ineffective people are at dealing with sticky situations and hard-to-handle people," he said. "I'm only there one week a month and a lot of times when we have a difficult resident, I'm the one who says we've got to deal with this situation and pushed them to deal with it.

"I've got equipping and training in dealing with people that I would not have otherwise. I've developed the emotional intelligence to handle those kinds of things."

If you're looking at your career choices and feeling discouraged that you didn't start out putting God first, don't let the devil keep you bottled up. Ask God to show the way through.

"'Seek first his kingdom and his righteousness and these things will be added to you' still works," Jeff added. "At this age you have more experience, more know-how, and you're in a better position to work from than you've ever had.

"Don't just leave because you're burned out. That's the wrong way to approach this. Ask God, 'Show me how to serve and modify my career.' We're still very young with a lot of life to live. We can have a lot of effect for the Lord. There's hope."

Section 3: Potential Outcomes

When asked why he wanted to ascend Mount Everest, British mountaineer George Mallory commented, "Because it's there."[5] Spiritual climbers could answer similarly—there's a life waiting for me that I want more than anything else.

As you give the earthly sources of your identity to God you will notice definite changes in a number of areas, each covered by a chapter in this section: home life, ministry, and yourself.

Before you begin this part of the book, start with a prayer something like this: Lord, help me envision the life you want for me as if it already existed, so that I can have the motivation to keep pursuing it no matter what.

Home Life

If someone were to ask, "What does God want you to do?" your first reaction would probably be in the context of career. Perhaps you'd think about hobbies or service opportunities. But would home life surface as an area of Spirit-led engagement?

While many acknowledge that family is a vital aspect of God's plan for their lives, the idea that God would have a specific will for their home life seems foreign. People don't think that way. Their first thoughts about a master scheme drift toward vocation and leaving a mark on the broader society. But few things make more of a difference than the way a person conducts herself in the domestic sphere.

The bigger world *will* notice if my kids are respectful, have fun and know how to give to others. The bigger world *will* observe if my marriage is marked by commitment, tenderness, truth, and joy. The bigger world *will* be touched by my family's unity, love, and commitment to the Great Commission.

In view of all this, I have an admission. I've spent a lot of time with my wife and kids: we do ministry together, take one or two vacations each year, share a family meal every day, have a picnic in the living room every Sunday night, play games, go swimming, etc. I enjoy all of that and believe that God has a specific role for me in the lives of Julia and my three kids, David, Bethany and Mark. But I also love to write.

There are days when I know it's the Lord's will for me to tappity-tap at my computer screen and forge ideas into sentences and paragraphs. I enjoy wordsmithery; I love expressing the abstract with ink-on-paper declarations. This is what I was made to do. Yet, even as I find satisfaction and meaning from writing, this is an incomplete landscape. And I know it.

• • • •

Family Life and Famous Bible People

• • • •

The Bible does have a lot to say about family life. Think about this interesting statement God makes about Abraham, the father of the Jews:

> For I have chosen him, so that he will direct his children and his household after him to keep the way of the LORD by doing what is right and just, so that the LORD will bring about for Abraham what he has promised him.
>
> GENESIS 18:19 (NIV)

God connects the keeping of his promise to Abraham, first stated in Genesis 12, with Abraham faithfully leading his family about knowing and following God. Abraham was a busy guy! How could God place this expectation on such a powerful, significant person? But that's the expectation.

There's also Job, who had seven sons and three daughters. The beginning of his story notes,

> His sons used to take turns holding feasts in their homes, and they would invite their three sisters to eat and drink with them. When a period of feasting had run its course, Job would send and have them purified. Early in the morning he would sacrifice a burnt offering for each of them, thinking, "Perhaps my children have sinned and cursed God in their hearts." This was Job's regular custom.
>
> JOB 1:4–5 (NIV)

What a great dad! And that last line is telling—this wasn't just the occasional, "Hey, I haven't really done anything for the kids lately, so I better do this" response. Watching out for his kids spiritually was normally on the radar screen for Job.

We know that Abraham and Job were both men of means with big responsibilities. But number one for both these fellows was their home life and particularly the spiritual well being of their families.

An example in the negative would be King David's relationship with Absalom. David did not handle things very well with his deceitful, handsome, and charismatic son. He didn't deal decisively with Absalom's murder of Amnon (see 2 Samuel 13). When he called Absalom back from exile he refused to see him for two years. Absalom eventually dethrones Dad and starts a civil war. Talk about the far-reaching consequences of family dysfunction! If only David had taken better care of things at home.

Then there's the command given by Moses,

> These commandments that I give you today are to be upon your hearts. Impress them on your children. Talk about them when you sit at home and when you walk along the road, when you lie down and when you get up.
>
> DEUTERONOMY 6:6–7 (NIV)

Of all the ways I can spend my time, nothing is as critical as advocating God's moral and mission priorities with my family. Am I asking my family about people they hope to talk with about Jesus? Am I talking about this like a priority or just an add-on? Are weekend plans centered on the question, "Whom does God want us to be with?" Am I asking my spouse about how things are going with the Lord? Do we talk frequently about character areas and trust issues that God is pressing in our lives? Do we raise those questions with the kids?

This recommends a very healthy and regular prayer life. How can I sense what the Lord's doing if I'm not talking with God? How can I detect his leading about whether to give a time out or talk with Johnny, about whether to go fishing or play basketball with Mike, about whether to discuss the themes in a TV show or just watch with Marie? God knows the way to go—I need to ask him already!

• • • •

A Moment with Dave Howard

• • • •

Even for the extremely committed Christian man or woman, God's call in the area of family needs attention.

I met Dave Howard several years ago at Cedar Campus, a retreat and training center in the Upper Peninsula of Michigan run by InterVarsity Christian Fellowship (IVCF). Dave was missions director for IVCF from 1968 to 1977 and coordinated the Urbana Missions Conventions in 1973 and 1976. Prior to his time at IVCF he worked with Latin America Mission in Costa Rica and Colombia.

Dave has quite a spiritual pedigree. His college roommate and best man at his wedding was Jim Elliot, a fellow Wheaton College graduate. Jim and four other young missionaries were murdered in 1956 by the Huaorani Indians, then known as the Auca, along a lonely strip of sand bordering an Ecuadoran river. The five were immortalized in the book *Through Gates of Splendor*, written by Jim's wife Elisabeth. Elisabeth is Dave's sister.

Dave continues to vigorously and regularly ask the question, "What does God want me to do?" even though he's now in his late seventies. But he admits he should have wrestled with that question more regarding family life during his middle years.

"I am seventy-eight years old and have been in mission work for over half a century," Dave said. "My wife Phyllis and I went to Latin America in 1953, and the rest of my life has been involved in missions. I have had a lot of 'success' in the eyes of the world of Christians, and I can be thankful for this. But what many people do not know is that I neglected my family for far too much of that time."

Dave was a product of his time, the post World War II generation. "I was in college from 1945 to 1949," he said. "We were hearing ringing challenges for missions in military terms such as, 'Our boys went overseas for two, three, four years to defend the world for democracy. Can we do *less* in the army of the Lord?' So my generation responded whole heartedly to the call for 'Sacrifice!' This was a big word in our vocabulary.

"If you ever read *The Journals of Jim Elliot* you will find frequent references to 'sacrifice' and 'death' and 'pouring out our blood on the altar for the sake of the Lord,' etc. etc. This was how we were thinking in those days."

Dave is describing the mindset of a spiritual warrior. This is very admirable and also clearly scriptural (2 Timothy 2:3–4, Ephesians 6:11). However, we engage an enemy on several fronts simultaneously, including the home. Dave's youngest son, Michael, was a casualty.

"When he was about thirteen he turned knowingly and deliberately away from the Lord," Dave said. "After he had come back, at least partially, I asked what caused him to throw over all he had learned at home. His reply cut me more deeply than almost anything I ever heard in my life. He said, 'I did not have a father when I needed him.'

"I will carry the pain of that statement to my grave," Dave added. "Nothing in my life was ever remotely as difficult to handle, until my wife Phyllis died suddenly and unexpectedly in 2003. That event was even worse. But the pain of 'losing' my son, and knowing that I was largely to blame, can never be recovered. Thankfully he and I have a good relationship now."

Dave's honesty about his failure shows one thing very clearly: this is about Jesus, not us. God's grace covers our mistakes—thank God! And he does provide a rich array of opportunities to learn and grow. But you can still miss things, as Dave admitted. That's why this discussion about God's direction for my life must include the home.

Even in view of Dave's regrets, he and his wife Phyllis did a pretty decent job of raising kids with the right priorities:

Their oldest boy, David Jr., is dean at Bethel Theological Seminary in St. Paul, MN teaching Old Testament Hebrew. He is also a former president of the Evangelical Theological Society.

Second child Stephen is a pilot with American Airlines, flying international routes to South America and Europe, and, as Dave explained, "Witnessing faithfully in his marketplace." According to Dave, Stephen is a first officer and has intentionally stayed in that post.

"If he moves up to captain, he starts at the bottom of the pile with far less flexibility in choosing his schedules," Dave said. "He is determined to give time to his three boys, ages fifteen, thirteen, and eleven, and his wife, even though he makes less money."

Beth is happily married in North Carolina, after a tragic divorce from a pastor who was unfaithful to her. She's actively reaching out to women and children in her hometown, especially to those in the Hispanic community.

Michael lives in Wheaton, IL with his wife and kids and works for Hong Kong Singapore Banking Corporation as a manager in computer operations.

"He makes sure that he gives time to his children," Dave said. "Probably his experience as a teenager who 'did not have a father when he needed him' challenges him to be the kind of father his children need."

• • • •

Surprises at Home

• • • •

Being the person God wants me to be at home has involved more than I had guessed. He has sprung interesting surprises on me as I've tried to obey his leading on the home front.

I cook now and then, and one of my favorite meals is breakfast for dinner. The kids get involved too. The whole process can resemble a massive mess hall operation—Bethany makes the pancakes, Mark cracks the eggs, Bethany gets the bacon, Mark scrambles the eggs, David sets the table.

Pretty soon the kitchen is looking like a scene from a situation comedy, but the kids and I have worked together to make a darn good meal. And it's one of those meals where no one complains partly because everyone's had a hand in making it (sometimes both hands!).

Here's the surprise part: my personality is engaged in a unique way during this far-flung operation—directing which kid to do what, showing one kid how to do something while counting on another kid to do their job, leading, managing, teaching and encouraging toward a definite end result: dinner.

I feel a great sense of satisfaction as I see everyone sitting around, quietly eating their food. Surprise! I didn't expect this from making a meal for my family. Why is that? Maybe it's because God is expert at blessing us when we're trying to serve others. He knows how to fill us as we're pouring ourselves out. And by that, I also mean the act of including others in serving too. There are times I'd much rather make a meal alone rather than engage the patience-stretching tension of watching my kids do things "imperfectly." When I surrender that desire for control and welcome their help, the Spirit begins the blessing bandwagon. Unless we're open to these happy revelations we will miss the richness of God's domestic agenda.

Making dinner may be difficult to imagine if you're a man. My dad cooked some, so this isn't a push for me. Some people were lucky to even see dad at the dinner table, let alone have him concoct a meal. For some ladies, life is so busy that taking the time for such a chaotic dinner endeavor with their children sounds like more work than their jobs.

Responding to the question "What does God want me to do?" may very well involve such "chaos." God may have me doing things with my spouse and children that I would have thought burdensome, boring or unimportant. He may have me love them in some practical fashion rather than doing something I want to do for them or for me.

My wife Julia experienced this during an afternoon off work. She took the kids school shopping and brought Grandma along to exchange a pair of shoes. She was fine with that plan, although she hoped to get her hair trimmed at the local salon. It didn't happen. So Julia remained a bit shaggy (although I thought she looked fine) but Grandma had new shoes, Mark was wearing new socks, and Bethany was stocked for class.

I appreciated Julia's conclusion about her "free time" that day. "Take advantage of what's in front of you," she said. "And it may not be the thing you want to do, but the serving thing that matters most."

I was running (okay, jogging!) in a 10K race with my friend Ken. There were people at various points of the race offering encouraging applause and cheering us to the finish line. At one of those junctures was a dad with his four or five kids. Ken turned to me and commented, "I think there's a lot of value in kids being a part of something like that, seeing how to give to others and be part of a community event." I agreed with a gasp of "right on" and then grunted my way another stride. But Ken was correct. Thank God for the dad who decided to spend his time that way on that day. He blessed many people by his decision and most of all he blessed his children.

• • • •

Welcome to Kid World!

• • • •

Have you ever voiced the dialogue between your daughter's prince and princess dolls before? If I'm asking God to use me at home, my sweet little girl may honor me with this highly significant request, "Can you play with me?" Or I might hear myself saying, "Hey son, instead of you going to Alex's house I thought we'd work on that model airplane you got for your birthday."

This must be pleasing to the Lord when parents love their children like this. Plus, we get the added benefit of building "kid credibility." When children hear their parents say "no" to something in this context, they understand from personal experience playing, doing projects together, and hanging out that mom and dad have their best interests in mind; we're more than rule-crazy joy-smashers. We're also more likely to have their attention when we instruct and lead.

If my interactions are limited to thirty minutes before bed I begin looking more like an umpire than a parent. Especially if during that half hour I'm asked to adjudicate a dispute or back up the spouse on an earlier behavior ruling. Even though I'm with David, Bethany and Mark quite a bit, there are still times when I become Umpire Dad because we've just been crazy busy and I haven't had the time to walk alongside them much.

Getting into my kids' world will certainly help me avoid "exasperating" them, as I'm commanded *not* to do in Ephesians 6:4. "Instead, bring them up in the training and instruction of the Lord," Paul goes on to say.

Training and teaching kids takes time. It requires being with them, letting them see how I deal with life, how I have fun, sharing how my Christian beliefs influence decision making. Altering my lifestyle and schedule may be the very thing required so I have the time to transfer my life in Christ to them.

What are some ways to know if your kids are getting enough of you in their lives? Think and pray about the following list of questions:

Can my children name my favorite color? This is customary little kid conversation. If they don't know, I may not be hanging with them enough. By the way, do they know my birthday (at least the month), whether I like pizza or not, whether I was a nerd, jock, or student government type in high school? That last one's for the older kids, but you get the point. My teens should know what kind of adolescent I was.

Have I ever smelled the nap of the carpet in my house? Okay, maybe some don't have carpet—that's no loophole! Getting into my kids' world will mean wrestling, setting up toy figures, and playing a board game—on the floor. Children spend a lot of time in the lower twenty-four to thirty-six inches of every room of the house. If I hope to influence them the way God desires I need to get down there too.

Have I ever read the Peter Rabbit, Winnie the Pooh, or Dr. Seuss books? Every adult should read *Green Eggs and Ham* as a rite of passage into parenthood.

Have I read the Bible with my kids? Nowadays you can find Bibles for every conceivable life stage, from board books for toddlers to comic book Bibles for the elementary years. There are tween and teen-oriented Bibles with interesting sidebar application material. Reading through and talking about the Bible should be standard stuff for the family that's trying to answer the question "What does God want us to do?"

Have I ever held my baby's head while he/she was puking? When I say baby I mean that in the broadest sense—the sixteen-year-old is still my baby. If I haven't held a head, have I at least done one or more of the following: filled a vaporizer, placed a thermometer where it needed to be placed, slept or at least laid down in the same bed with a sick child, sat with a kid in an emergency room waiting for x-rays, handed out ibuprofen, acetaminophen, or a cough and cold medicine?

Do my children know my friends and vice versa? If I aspire to having a Great Commission family, then my kids should know my friends; they should know if they're Christians or not; they should know something about them. And it should work the opposite direction too. Can I name my son or daughter's friends? Do I know where those friends are at with Jesus? Do I know how to encourage Johnny and Susie to invest in those friendships for Jesus' purposes?

Have I ever told my kids I was wrong? Have I apologized to them when they were right? Have they heard me confess my goofs or when I treated someone badly? Have they heard me admit my failure to God and affirm his forgiveness for my moral errors?

•   •   •   •

Total Experience

•   •   •   •

Lying about on a lazy afternoon, reading the comics with the preschooler, pushing junior on the tire swing, showing the kids how to bake cookies or build a tree house, taking a walk with my better half and talking about something besides who's taking which child to which extracurricular activity.

You may have these interactions at home, and I pray that you do. But the answer to the question, "What does God want me to do at home?" may have greater outcomes.

For example, surrendering my current lifestyle to God may lead to an alteration of household responsibilities. A 1998 University of Cincinnati study showed that working women still handle most of the cooking, vacuuming, ironing, and dish washing.[6] Having more time for these chores will be a blessing for women. But domestic duties may be one of Dad's crucibles for transformation.

I hadn't seriously thought about washing dishes or folding laundry much before marriage. I did my share of both as a single man, but cleaning the kitchen as a normal part of everyday life had never entered my mind. And yet I'm definitely the kitchen cleaner guy. I didn't see that one coming. But this is also part of the answer to the question, "What does God want me to do?"

Let me respond quickly to the more incredulous, who are thinking, out loud perhaps, *Does this guy seriously think that God wants him to wash dishes? Are you kidding!* Yeah, washing dishes as part of God's plan may be a tough idea to digest. Let me go on a bit.

If doing dishes conflicts with my definition of self then I'll never consider washing dishes. If cleaning toilets doesn't fit the way I look at myself then it won't happen. But identity is not task driven, it's God given. I have to start with myself as a sinner who's rescued from judgment by God's loving action in the world. Then following the example of Christ becomes more important than whether a certain household task is "below me."

If my overriding desire is to see my family pursue God's priorities, then doing dishes or cleaning toilets or helping with math homework may be a way I free up time for them to serve. By helping with domestic stuff I provide Julia breathing room to work on a small group Bible study. By helping kids with homework I give her the chance to call a sister in Christ. This is reciprocal—there are days when I need someone to "wash my feet" so I can hang out with a buddy or witness to a friend or just get some down time.

And what about that washing-the-feet incident in John 13? That wasn't a respected job in Jesus' time. But no one questioned Jesus' strength or authority and neither did he, so he washed the dirty, mucky toes, heels, and arches of his confused disciples. And Jesus offered them a challenge:

Now that I, your Lord and Teacher, have washed
your feet, you also should wash one another's feet.
I have set you an example that you should do as I
have done for you. I tell you the truth, no servant is
greater than his master, nor is a messenger greater
than the one who sent him. Now that you know
these things, you will be blessed if you do them.

JOHN 13:14–17 (NIV)

Here's an interesting observation that precedes this
incident. John, one of the guys whose feet Jesus sani-
tized, writes,

Jesus knew the Father had put all things under his
power, and that he had come from God and was
returning to God; so he got up from the meal, took
off his outer clothing, and wrapped a towel around
his waist.

JOHN 13:3–4 (NIV)

Jesus knew who he was. He didn't need to obtain
power or act like powerful people acted. He was powerful already. He also knew where he belonged and
was confident about his relationship with the Father.
Because of this he was free to serve in a way that fulfilled the Father's mission, in spite of societal conven-
tion or others' expectations. The normal life was not
enough for Jesus; only an astounding life would do.

This merges with Jesus' observations about leadership in Mark chapter ten. He says there,

You know that those who are regarded as rulers of
the Gentiles lord it over them, and their high offi-
cials exercise authority over them. Not so with you.
Instead, whoever wants to become great among you
must be your servant, and whoever wants to be first

165

must be slave of all. For even the Son of Man did not come to be served, but to serve, and to give his life as a ransom for many.

MARK 10:42–45 (NIV)

These truths, more than the words of society, parents, siblings or friends, should guide my thinking about home life. Because of the changes I make, I will become wealthier emotionally and spiritually. With this truth as my guide, I'll facilitate my family giving their lives away in an eternally-meaningful manner.

Julia puts together photo albums bulging at the seams each year, filled with big and little moments of joy, domestic and otherwise, mostly afforded by trusting God with who we are and what we do. If I don't let his word search me on this point, I'll miss that joy and miss a significant dimension of God's purpose.

Ministry

Maybe this section of the book should have its own slogan, something like "Ministry—it's not just for ministers anymore!" For so long the church has held this distinction between the professional ministers who take care of everyone and the average ordinary believer or nonbeliever who receives their efforts. Having paid people is not the problem; seeing the paid person as the only one who's supposed to build God's kingdom is the problem.

God's intention is that all Christians become influencers for Jesus in this world, whether it's with people I know or people I don't know, people who have a relationship with God and those who don't:

> Let us not become weary in doing good, for at the proper time we will reap a harvest if we do not give up. Therefore, as we have opportunity, let us do

good to *all* people, especially to those who belong to the *family of believers.*

GALATIANS 6:9–10 (NIV, EMPHASIS ADDED)

I contend that, in the broadest sense, ministry is "doing good" because of Jesus. And, my first thought, not my second or third thought, should be "how can I arrange my life so I'm as available as possible for service to others." Granted, part of this is a mindset which I can adopt right now regardless of my life situation.

The Good Samaritan was just as busy as the priest and the Levite, the two other characters in the story. But the Samaritan did more than rubber neck at the site of the accident. "He went to [the injured man] and bandaged his wounds, pouring on oil and wine. Then he put the man on his own donkey, took him to an inn and took care of him," Jesus said (Luke 10:34, NIV). He saw the injured man, felt compassion, and helped him.

But on the other hand, if my life is so crowded with other things, like my kids' extra-curricular activities (and oh boy, can those add up quickly), that I hardly have brain and heart space for compassion, then maybe I need to evaluate the way I'm living. If I'm not doing as much good as I ought, it's not for lack of opportunity.

When it comes to doing good because of Jesus there's plenty of flexibility. Some ministries are quite structured, with nonprofit tax status, middle and upper management, fundraising campaigns, pie chart diagrams and sticky memos with the ministry's name, while others are more ad hoc and on the fly. But the end goal is doing good because of Jesus, whether the ministry is highly organized or one person responding in the moment.

Ministry *ought* to be something God's people are thinking about, or at least aware of, all the time. "As we have opportunity" is the phrase Paul uses. This implies a state of mind—that I'm staying on the alert in a steady, front-of-my-consciousness way for those chances to let the Lord's kindness shine through. The need for stream-of-life, off-the-cuff prayer becomes obvious.

Ron Reece is a friend of mine who lives this out through his knowledge of automobiles. Earlier in life he owned a used car lot and got to know the ins and outs of a car's engine pretty well.

Ron, who lives in New Orleans, has equipped the back end of his van with a tool crib so he can stop and help stranded motorists. He's got wrenches and hose clamps and fan belts and transmission fluid in there, along with myriads of other stuff that a volunteer emergency mechanic would need. When he sees someone stuck on the highway he pulls over and offers to check things out. These folks will often ask Ron who he's working for or assume he's with the highway department, but he will quite humbly say something like, "I just felt like God wanted me to help you." To which these people will respond with a simple thanks and a confused yet grateful expression.

Ron has organized his life around being ready for opportunities like that. First time he told me about this I thought, *How excellent!* I was especially impressed because I only have a confidence level of three on a scale of ten when it comes to solving car problems. But Ron's confidence level is nine and he knows he's got something special to offer other human beings in need. Because of Jesus, he's offering what he's got.

Offering what I've got is all Jesus is asking for. Some

of us are great at entertaining and having people over for dinner. That's a tremendous service and something God says all Christians ought to do. Some of us are fantastic listeners. Others know how to wire a house or install a fence post. Some people are knowledgeable about legal things or medical things or computer things or about dealing with government bureaucracy.

My friend Virginia Avery is lickety-split with answers about getting government help; she also knows how to tool around the Internet to find answers on everything from the cheapest computer to how to sign up for Medicare. I thank God for her availability and desire to help this way.

Then there are personal abilities that are gifts from God. These are described in places like 1 Corinthians 12:7–11. That paragraph talks about people who have supernatural wisdom. A friend of mine, Lynne Jones, has this ability. She will be the first person to tell you she has plenty of character issues God's working on. But there are moments when she makes a perceptive comment about a person or situation and you feel all goose-pimply and inspired because you know that insight was Holy Spirit-powered. That's the gift of wisdom.

Whatever I have—whether it's a knowledge base, an area of expertise, or a spiritual gift—I need to acknowledge what I've got. Then, give it back to God (it's his anyway), ask that he use me to give it away to others and look for occasions to do so. That's the soul of Galatians 6:9–10.

That won't be the end of it, however. God will also stretch my criteria for serving, beyond what I find comfortable and normal for me. Most people find me easy going and easy to talk to. I listen fairly well, try to keep eye contact, have a decent degree of patience, and can ask questions that go a little deeper to show people I'm paying attention. I try to do this honestly and care for people this way. Some people, who find it difficult to open up otherwise, will open up to me. I'm glad God uses me like this.

But that's not good enough for God. He's always aiming for something I'm not yet. He and I always seem to hit a crossroads.

For example, it can be hard for me to disagree with someone or correct another person when he's wrong. I much prefer being the likeable, attentively head-nodding, affirming guy. But, right there in Ephesians 4:15, I find my nemesis—"Speak the truth in love." Can't I just love and if truth gets in there, fine? No, ministering to others will often mean speaking truth in a way that puts me at risk emotionally and relationally for the good of the listener. And this is a place where God is challenging me today as I try to serve someone else.

Let's return to the touchstone passage, Galatians 6:9–10. In that section, Paul talks about caring for family, but he's not thinking about Mom, Dad, and the munchkins. God wants us to be concerned about the *family of believers*, which most definitely includes my spouse and children, but also any who know Jesus as savior.

Now, as most families go, there's a bigger, more expansive definition, like all those second cousins, third cousins, and fifteenth cousins you see once every ten years at the reunion. Then there's the more immediate crowd—Grandma and Grandpa, Mom and Dad, brothers, sisters, aunts and uncles, and first cousins you see more often.

As Christians we have a large, expansive family, all of us related through Jesus, who is the "head" of the whole clan (see Colossians 1:18). Then we have the smaller units, our congregations, which are still too unwieldy for the description "close knit." Even "small" churches have memberships of several hundred. There ought to be even smaller units—the part of the family we know the best, the "relatives" about whom we know some of the more icky details of their lives and vice versa, whom we love and have meaningful contact with in a regular fashion, weekly at least, usually more.

Let me share several intriguing verses. They're located in the last chapters of two New Testament letters, so no wonder they might escape notice. Honestly, how many sermons have you heard on the goodbye chapters? Here they are: "The churches in the province of Asia send you greetings. Aquila and Priscilla greet you warmly in the Lord, and so does the church that meets at their house" (1 Corinthians 16:19, NIV). "Give my greetings to the brothers at Laodicea, and to Nympha and the church in her house" (Colossians 4:15, NIV).

Aquila and Priscilla had a church meeting at their house. Big house! Same with Nympha. Her place must have been huge!

Yes, they had small to medium-size gatherings of believers meeting in their homes but, interestingly, Paul doesn't call them "fellowship groups" or "Bible studies" but uses the same word that gets used in the Bible for the whole collection of believers all over the world— the church. They just happen to be smaller expressions of the "church" but still the church nonetheless.

It's kind of like chocolate. I might take a piece of a candy bar but that doesn't mean my piece becomes something else because it's only a portion of the larger chunk. It's still chocolate, no matter the size. That's how it is with the church.

Two or three, gathered in the name of Jesus, are the church. Two or three thousand, gathered in his name, are the church. I might not get to experience the full range of the Spirit's divine enablement in a church of three, but it doesn't happen much in a church of 3,000 either, unless that large gathering is broken off into component "families" meeting to love each other and carry out the Great Commission together.

Which brings me to another reason for restructuring my life—discipleship.

One of the greatest ways I can minister to another is by investing my life in his. This is one of the most compelling reasons for making time for my family: so I can spend enough time with them to know where their spiritual passions lie, teach them what God's been teaching me, talk honestly about character problems, study the Bible, pray for and reach out to those who don't know Jesus, and spend time with those who want to know him better.

People are God's priority. For the last twenty years, this has been one of the major ways God has reshaped and reconfigured my convictions and beliefs.

I've been involved in small group Bible study for a long time. But my thinking has changed the last four or five years. I use to think, *Grow an interesting group and people will start flocking to it and then you can start another group or have a really big meeting.* But the path to that aspiration, in my mind, went through having really captivating, graphically-illustrated teachings and unique, exciting social events.

Both of these have a place in carrying out God's work. However, the Lord's first priority is individuals and he wants us to interact with and love individuals in a deep way. That takes time. Time that can seem, how should I put it, hmm … not well spent, and not very enthralling, and in fact, a little confusing and sometimes absolutely baffling. But that's the nature of discipleship. There are times when it's also exciting and deeply rewarding.

Earlier in the book, Doug Patch, formerly a trainer of world-class track and field athletes, talked about attending the Goodwill Games in Russia. On his flight home, he tried conjuring up the pageantry and bigger-than-life emotions of this world-stage event. But his mind kept flowing back to something even more profound—the opportunity he had to help a young guy, who'd just come to faith, grow in his relationship with God.

I've been as guilty as anyone of looking at Jesus' ministry in terms of the big numbers. The feeding of the 5000. The multitudes coming to be healed. The crowds, like sheep without a shepherd, herding around him wherever he went. But, as we may know, the main thing going on with Jesus was his efforts with this small group of guys, twelve total, that he did everything with—eating meals, walking around the countryside, discussing the nature of the kingdom of God, confronting demons, healing sick people, teaching, visiting people's homes. Yes, and scolding them when necessary.

And boy, were there some ups and downs, such as the Zebedee brothers asking to be co-rulers with Jesus. What an outlandishly selfish move. Or the same guys asking Jesus about calling down fire on some Samaritans. Not only were they power hungry, they were vindictive too.

Then you have the whole Peter 'get behind me Satan' episode. Peter thought he knew the will of God better than the Lord of the universe. Glad I've never done that. Or the time he denied even knowing Jesus, not once but three times, selling out his loyalty to the Lord in order to protect himself. I can't say I would have done any better.

The whole bunch shared an absolute cluelessness about Jesus' main mission during his first coming. You can see Jesus' exasperation with these men in places like John 14:

> Philip said, "Lord, show us the Father and that will be enough for us." Jesus answered: "Don't you know me, Philip, even after I have been among you such a long time? Anyone who has seen me has seen the Father. How can you say, 'Show us the Father'?"
>
> JOHN 14:8–9 (NIV)

Even so, this is where Jesus put his prime time: not in the miracles or the Sermon on the Mount or the confrontations with the religious leaders. All these had value, but not the same value as the time spent caring for, teaching, correcting, listening, modeling, challenging, and loving Peter, John, James, and the rest.

This part of what Jesus did was so critical that it ranks behind his death and resurrection in order of purpose for his life. You gather that from his last long prayer, recorded in John 17. He comments: "I have brought you glory on earth by completing the work you gave me to do" (John 17:4, NIV).

And the first thing he mentions regarding that work? "I have revealed you to those whom you gave me out of the world. They were yours; you gave them to me and they have obeyed your word." (John 17:6, NIV)

The energy expended on these guys, day and night, transformed them. Note Jesus' observation later in chapter seventeen, "I have given them your word and the world has hated them, for they are not of the world any more than I am of the world" (John 17:14, NIV).

So being around Jesus and hearing what he had to say changed these guys into people with different values than the world. That's why the world hated them. By hanging out with Jesus and receiving what he said they became "other worldly" people.

That others noticed the change shows up in the book of Acts. Luke records in chapter four about the Sanhedrin, a first-century Jewish equivalent to our Supreme Court,

> When they saw the courage of Peter and John and realized that they were unschooled, ordinary men, they were astonished and they took note that these men had been with Jesus.
>
> ACTS 4:13 (NIV)

That's all great. These guys got to be with the Son of God twenty-four hours a day, seven days a week. I hope that would touch me in a pervasive, all-encompassing way. So I'm fine with that. But then Jesus says we should go out and do the same:

> All authority in heaven and on earth has been given to me. Therefore go and make disciples of all nations, baptizing them in the name of the Father and of the Son and of the Holy Spirit, and teaching them to obey everything I have commanded you.
>
> MATTHEW 28:18–20 (NIV)

What possibly could I offer another Christian?

Well, that may be a very telling question. At this point, maybe not much. Maybe I should be more in the position of someone discipled—a student of God under the guidance and direction of someone further along than me. Aim for a discipleship triad, where you receive from another but are also helping another believer to mature. That's a really good growth place for everyone.

For some, this will sound like a conversation in a foreign language. Their churches may have relegated "discipleship" to the Sunday school class. In fact, maybe that's what their church calls adult Sunday school—discipleship 101, or disciples in action or something like that. Now, there's no question a person can learn from that setting, especially if they have a gifted teacher who has some tread wear from following the Lord and his truth.

But there is something special about this interaction between two or three people meeting together for the intention of knowing Jesus better. There's a value-added dimension, which makes the experience greater than it might appear to someone observing it. Kind of like watching someone drive a car.

There are certain things that make an automobile go—pistons, oil, gears, exhaust manifold, battery, starter, sparkplugs, etc. You can talk about all that very clinically, how when you press the accelerator it makes the engine spin at a certain RPM which produces so much energy and off you go. But that's not what the New York advertising guys sell—it's the feel of the engine humming, the thrill of accelerating, the sense of control as the wheels hug the road and you muscle through a curve. It's the gestalt of driving, which no manual can adequately describe.

And that's kind of what happens in discipleship.

Sometimes you don't even know or understand the fullness of what's happening while you're being with this other person. You just thought you were meeting Joanne and Rita at the coffee bar and talking about how to follow God. But then something else took charge and you met with God somehow too. And he moved things forward in all of your lives in a way you hadn't imagined. This is merely the realization of what Jesus promised in Matthew 18:20, "For where two or three come together in my name, there am I with them" (NIV).

And what is discipleship at its core? Two or three Christians coming together to become more like Jesus. Usually, there's one person who's more knowledgeable about the Bible and has more experience trusting God's truth and relying on the Holy Spirit in real-life situations. Sometimes those involved are at a similar level. Whatever the mix, the point is helping each other become more like Jesus in the way we think and the way we live. Here's a good summary of what's involved:

> We proclaim him, admonishing and teaching everyone with all wisdom, so that we may present everyone perfect in Christ. To this end I labor, struggling with all his energy, which so powerfully works in me.
>
> COLOSSIANS 1:28–29 (NIV)

When Paul talks perfect, he means completeness, wholeness or totalness. It's similar to that place we aim for with our kids. When our children go out on their own, having landed that first job and having signed a lease for their first apartment, we don't imagine they're perfect. But our job is done. Hopefully we've raised children who go potty on their own, read books, follow instructions, learn independently, drive a car, hold a job, feed themselves, pay bills, love Jesus, love others, and share the Gospel. The analogy doesn't transfer exactly, but that's what we aim for in discipleship.

Can this other person walk with God independently? Do they hold the core truths of Christianity with conviction—that Jesus was born of a virgin, was both God and man, that he died and rose again and his sacrifice and resurrection are necessary for our salvation from God's judgment? Do they read the Bible on their own, pray on their own, read spiritual-growth literature on their own, seek Jesus out about most to all aspects of life. Are they committed to Christian community, understand they have something crucial to give to others and do something about it? Is their interaction with God the source of that activity?

Is this person aware of major character issues—they're selfish with their time, they're rude, they're uncaring, they lie—and trying to cooperate with God to become someone different? Do they care that neighbors, friends, sports buds, hobby pals don't know Jesus? Are they praying for these people, arranging time to be with those people, asking God to be a good friend to these folks and to open doors naturally for spiritual conversations? Are they taking the risk to inform others how to know God? Are they now pouring themselves into another Christian and helping that person toward totalness?

How does discipleship help all these things happen? Part of it has to do with the way I structure my time with someone. I'll offer this grid, which comes from Gary DeLashmutt, one of the best mentors I know. Dennis McCallum and he started Xenos Christian Fellowship, a church of 150 plus outreaching Christian communities in Columbus, Ohio. Gary says he tries to get four elements in his time with someone:

• Counseling - the goal here is becoming a more godly man or woman, someone whose life is showing greater signs of the Lord's righteousness and goodness and love. This happens as you listen to the other person talk about his life; you ask questions, trying to gain understanding and then encourage or exhort, depending on the situation, to think about what following God in that situation would look like; you also talk about your spiritual struggles and successes in real life situations and how God is changing you. This includes honesty about your sin areas and discussion of how to cooperate with God for change.

• Coaching - here you're trying to help the person develop their own ministry. You might talk about how they engaged or didn't engage other people at a recent small group fellowship you're both a part of; you might offer encouragement and show excitement for how something they said or did during the group was beneficial to you or others; you should also talk about non-Christians this person knows, whether they're praying for these folks and trying to spend time with them and how their time with that person is going. As this person begins meeting with someone else for discipleship your conversations should include how that's going.

• Study - you're trying to help this person learn how to study the Bible for themselves and develop a love for it and show them how to integrate God's truth into their framework for viewing life. You could do this by actually reading through a book of the Bible during your time together, discussing what you read, looking at Bible commentaries and other resources to gain understanding. Or you might do the reading and researching before you meet so you're ready for the discussion part when you come together.

• Prayer - pray with the person, show them that prayer is something anyone can do, that he or she can go to God anytime and talk in a normal, open, friendly manner. Show them what it's like to acknowledge God's greatness; admit your sin failures; make requests for yourself, your family, your home group friends; pray for non-Christian friends to see their sin and need for the Gospel; and ask for chances to talk with them.

I feel I still have much to learn about discipleship but I'll share with you how a recent time with my friends Mark and Kenny went. First of all, we met in a restaurant where my niece Jeni was manager.

We started out talking about house repairs, because Jeni had asked me if I knew someone that did that kind of work. Very practical stuff. Then we moved on to a book we're reading on conflict resolution. The chapter was on bringing in a third party to help settle differences when a one-on-one confrontation has failed. We talked about Matthew 18, which the author had centered his discussion on. I was struck at how far God calls us to go to make peace, and how that's much further than I would go naturally on my own. Mark and Kenny agreed.

Next we talked about those guys praying for and working toward having someone else to disciple before the end of the year. We talked about some guys Mark knows and the next steps he could take. We talked about Kenny praying for direction about who that might be in his life.

This led into a discussion about facing fear and

trusting the Lord to have your back as you move out to follow him. I referenced Isaiah 58:6–9a which makes this promise, "The glory of the LORD will be your rear guard. Then you will call, and the LORD will answer; you will cry for help, and he will say: Here am I" (Isaiah 58:8–9a, NIV).

I was trying to encourage them that as they pushed forward in this endeavor, God would protect them. We also talked about how the Lord integrates the multiple strands of our lives. Mark loves working with kids—he's been involved in basketball ministry and served as a reading tutor. How does discipling an adult fit in? God may very well bring a guy along who wants to grow spiritually and who also has an interest in children.

Along those lines we discussed 1 Corinthians 12:4–6,

> There are different kinds of gifts, but the same Spirit. There are different kinds of service, but the same Lord. There are different kinds of working, but the same God works all of them in all men.
>
> I CORINTHIANS 12:4–6 (NIV)

We ended the evening praying that God would reveal to us how Satan may try to derail our efforts to find other disciples; we prayed about specific people and situations we're facing; we praised God for his goodness and faithfulness. We did all that sitting around our little table. Then we said goodbye and off we went. All that took about two and a half hours on a Tuesday night.

Some of us may only have an hour or so on a Wednesday morning. Go with that. Although I think an hour and a half is about the minimum time needed, once a week. Some may have spouses who will need to be persuaded about this use of time. Pray for God's help and direction talking with them. But don't let up on the accelerator.

This process is God's prescription for totalness in Christ. I can hear Bible teachings about being forthright, but until a Christian friend comments to me, "You know, you seem to hold out on things. I hear one thing when we meet and then I hear other things through the grapevine." Then I have to look at a very real character issue in my life. Or, I can know that evangelism is important, but unless Mark or Kenny asks me, "So, did you set up lunch with Frank?" I can find it easy to let my zeal wane.

You might be intrigued about discipleship but also wondering, *How would I even begin?* Maybe you don't know anyone in your church discipling anyone else. Pray that God would show you a person, hopefully in your church but maybe not, who wants to grow in Christ in the ways described. When I prayed that a couple years ago God led me to my neighbor Mark, who was attending another church. And don't just pray that prayer once—be diligent. Pray it at least daily for a couple weeks. God will show you someone.

Here's the other part—I'm in the same home fellowship group with Mark and Kenny, and now also my neighbor Mark. God may want to take you and the person you're meeting with and begin to form a small community around you two—your spouses and children to start. You begin to hold a study with all of them. And then one of the non-Christian friends you're praying for will start to ask questions. You'll have her over for dinners and get together casually. Eventually she accepts your invite to check out your little community, after repeated invites. And away you go. That's why Jesus said the kingdom of God is like a mustard seed.

Because I've made myself more available to God, he will bring people around to make me more complete in Christ and whom I can help the same way. It's one of the premier ways I can "do good" during my span of years on earth. But it doesn't end at earth's doorstep: "For what is our hope, our joy, or the crown in which we will glory in the presence of our Lord Jesus when he comes? Is it not you? Indeed, you are our glory and joy (1 Thessalonians 2:19–20, NIV).

Paul gets excited at being in the presence of God and having these folks from southern Greece stand around him. And I don't think it had anything to do with baklava. He was excited because he loved them, he knew they would be in heaven with him some day, and he would see the pay off of his investment in human hearts. Here's the biggest, most compelling reason for rearranging my life—so there's someone, perhaps a myriad of someones, in heaven to greet me with bear hugs when the time comes.

Yourself

We all have identities. We have identities as members of a family—Mom, Dad, brother, sister. We have identities in our churches—Sunday school teacher, small group leader, kids' ministry volunteer, singer in the choir. And we have identities in other fields of endeavor too—hard charging third baseman on the softball team, creative and talented quilter, chatty and inquisitive book club member. We have identities as employees—hard working, punctual, comedian, decision maker.

We also have our identities as people, the way we like to fancy ourselves in the magnificent blueprint of life. Some of us see ourselves as go getters; others as teachers or coaches; some of us as analysts and evaluators; others as nurturers and comforters. Often times we're a combination of two or three, or maybe even four.

God has room for all our definitions of self but he

created the schematic. He can take me from where I'm at and shape me into the person he has in mind. Giving my current way of life to God is like saying, "Here I am Lord, change me!"

God loves to transform human beings. He knows exactly what kind of person I ought to be instead of the version I've settled on. There are things about me just waiting to be unleashed and discovered, but my adherence to a comfortable and predictable life keeps all that bottled up. Honestly, this desire for my peace is really disobedience to God's call.

This brings to mind a profound point Jesus made just a few days before his death, "I tell you the truth, unless a kernel of wheat falls to the ground and dies, it remains only a single seed. But if it dies, it produces many seeds" (John 12:24, NIV).

Jesus was referring to his upcoming crucifixion but he was also expressing a principle to apply. I can settle for being a seed—a shiny, beautiful, glorious seed—but in the end, only a seed. This, however, is not the purpose of a seed. A seed contains life. That life is meant to get out and be explosively and magnificently productive. That won't happen unless I put the seed in an environment that is mucky, messy and meant to foster decay, i.e. the dirt. God wants to bring life out of the shell; he wants to bring life out of the "shell" I'm living in too.

Jesus adds this perplexing but clarifying comment in verse 25, "The man who loves his life will lose it, while the man who hates his life in this world will keep it for eternal life" (John 12:25, NIV).

This doesn't have anything to do with self-loathing, but with knowing and following Jesus or preserving my "shell." Will I "love" the beautiful husk I'm living in or "hate" it and put myself in a place that's messy but will allow life to burst forth? When I hold open palms up to him, presenting my life as the only sensible response to his grace, I'm telling Jesus, "Put me in the mud Lord!"

•   •   •   •

Extreme God Makeovers

•   •   •   •

People who begin one way and end up something different. That's one of the most awesome features of the Bible to me.

Sure, we all go through metamorphoses in life. Life does that—you become wiser, not so naïve, a little more shrewd; you develop a longer view of how things happen; your physical appearance changes. But a real metamorphosis, where my identity and destiny change in a radical fashion—that is remarkable! Shepherd David becomes king of Israel. Insecure Gideon becomes a powerful leader. Beautiful Queen Esther risks her life to save her people. Then there's Jacob.

Jacob was a man's man. This guy had twelve sons— twelve sons! In many societies this would seal his identity as a "real" man, even though whether your baby is a boy or girl is a toss of the dice. Regardless, there are no questions about Jacob's manhood from the husbandry perspective.

He was also a man of means. According to the Scripture he had large herds of sheep, goats, cattle, donkeys, and camels, the equivalent in our day of being extremely well off.

Also according to the Bible, Jacob had the audacity to wrestle with the Lord. That's how he got his other name—Israel. Literally, it means one who wrestles with God. According to the story, found in Genesis 32, Jacob would not let go of the angel of the Lord until he got a blessing. He got a blessing but also a limp. So not only was he a wrestler, but he also had a sports injury.

But look at where Jacob started:

> The boys grew up, and Esau became a skillful hunter, a man of the open country, while Jacob was a quiet man, staying among the tents. Isaac, who had a taste for wild game, loved Esau, but Rebekah loved Jacob.
>
> GENESIS 25:27–28 (NIV)

Jacob was a homebody, a guy who liked to hang out "among the tents" (read: he was into the domestic thing, not the manly hunter-gatherer thing). He was also a momma's boy. We learn later in the story that Jacob was a cook. Not that there's anything wrong with being a good cook, but in our society, at least to some degree, that is still a function often associated with women.

I wonder if Jacob still cooked after becoming a tribal chieftain. I don't know. But he had it in him. We do know that he could still weave with the best of them (see Genesis 37:3).

Mark Patterson has been a U.S. Navy Midshipman and college professor and currently works as an electrical engineer. He can take apart and put together a car's engine, solve exotic math problems, run 5Ks and half-marathons, and remodel his house. He also loves to cook. And he's good at it. We never know what's in a person, even ourselves, but God does. Consider the Apostle John.

John was a physical guy—a fisherman, like a lot of the disciples, and he had a hot temper. Jesus nicknamed John and his brother James the "sons of thunder" (Mark

3:17). So John was Thunder Boy or Thunder Man, like a superhero. He, along with his brother, recommended Jesus torch a community of unfriendly Samaritans (Luke 9:54).

Then there's the episode described in Luke 10, when both brothers approached Jesus about sitting in places of power when he became king.

John was ambitious in a way applauded in American society—he knew he was associated with "The Man" but he had competition—the other disciples. So he and his brother concocted a pre-emptive strike strategy. John was a passionate, no-holds-barred ladder climber Donald Trump would have been proud of. John was the original "Apprentice."

But he was also the only disciple to show up at the crucifixion. And while he was there, Jesus gave John a special assignment:

> When Jesus saw his mother there, and the disciple whom he loved standing nearby, he said to his mother, "Dear woman, here is your son," and to the disciple, "Here is your mother." From that time on, this disciple took her into his home.
>
> JOHN 19:26–27 (NIV)

This is the same man who refers to the recipients of his first letter as "dear children." Not once, but nine times.

God also uses John to tell us something very succinct and important about himself—that he is love. Not a God who willy-nilly calls down fire on folks, or who seeks his own self-interest ahead of others, but who taught us what love really looks like.

So whether I'm a sensitive soul, a hard working breadwinner, a do-it-yourselfer, or an organizer with a slight hint of creativity, God's idea for me is completion, a total human being in Christ. That means he will work on spots where I am lacking.

Facing weakness and inadequacy is a big part of figuring out what God wants me to do. It's also a big reason why so many, including myself, have often settled for a caricature of personhood instead of the free-wheeling adventure ride God has in mind.

If I'm a nurturer, God may want me to become more forceful and assertive, to gain confidence in myself as a person who gets things done. If I'm more functional, God may have me work on talking with my kids or my spouse or my parents, or just talking with anyone, period. If I tend to talk about certain subjects, like work or sports, he may want me to discuss feelings, spiritual growth, fears, hopes, joys.

I will encounter areas that look like potential rock-slides. All my tendencies will say, "No way, I'll never do this" or "I'll never be a good communicator with my kids" or "I'll never know how to talk about my relationship with Jesus in an engaging way."

God is calling me to something unbelievable but it will mean honestly looking at myself and saying to God, "Change me, make me complete in Christ." Or as the psalmist puts it, "Search me, O God, and know my heart; test me and know my anxious thoughts. See if there is any offensive way in me, and lead me in the way everlasting" (Ps. 139:23–24, NIV).

• • • •

Renovating My Emotional Life

• • • •

Taking care of my kids has been a unique path toward greater spiritual maturity for me. I have faced identity issues such as what it means to be a man, am I living a meaningful life, am I wasting my time, and whose opinion matters to me most. I'm not sure I would have faced these questions otherwise. God refines character in the crucible, but different crucibles for different metals.

One of those changes has been my emotional life. I've seen this at work in my friendship with Mark Janicki.

Mark went through a lot several years ago. His workplace moved twenty miles; his wife Elaine went through major surgery; he became a grandpa for the first time; and his own father went through double bypass surgery with serious implications for Mark and his family.

It's normal for me to see Mark through the lens of "friend I study the Bible and do ministry with." Not that we wouldn't talk about all the other features of his life, but God's been showing me how he wants to grow the empathy component of my life by just being there for people in whatever way I need to be.

Mark is not just a Bible study man or witnessing guy, but he's also a son dealing with heavy emotions about his father, a grandpa really excited about his grandkids, a husband who's concerned about his wife's health. He's multi-faceted and God has shown me I need to be more of a whole friend, not just a partial friend. So I've tried to spend more time sorting out how things with dad are affecting him in all areas of life, including his relationship with God. Through trying to learn more about his role as a grandparent and the importance of his little granddaughter in his life, I have visited her and his daughter Michelle.

God wants to see emotional growth in all of us.

Maybe I'm the type of person who's governed by my feelings more than my head. God definitely wants to work on that. There's the old illustration showing the "train of faith." The engine of the train is "fact," the middle car "faith," and the caboose "feelings." The idea is this: I should learn and dwell on the facts of my relationship with Christ and who God is and what he commands. Then as I act in trust on those truths with the help of the Spirit, regardless and sometimes against my feelings, he will supply confirming feelings in the wake of those steps.

It can work in reverse too. If I'm not very in touch with the emotional side of life, then God may show me steps to grow in this area. Maybe he nudges me, "Go ask your friend how he's doing, especially since his chin is on the floor." So, I go up to George and say, "So, how you doin'? You're not looking too good." Such questions could be followed by looking-in-the-eyes listening and more inquiry before I start providing solutions, if I provide any at all.

Some of the best emotional relating in the whole Bible is recorded in the book of Job, though not a word is spoken. Eliphaz, Bildad, and Zophar visit their friend to encourage and comfort the roughed-up Job. But they're overwhelmed by what they find:

> When they saw him from a distance, they could hardly recognize him; they began to weep aloud, and they tore their robes and sprinkled dust on their heads. Then they sat on the ground with him for seven days and seven nights. No one said a word to him, because they saw how great his suffering was.
>
> JOB 2:12–13 (NIV)

Here was genuine mourning. The desire to problem-solve kicked in later as E, B, and Z speculated how badly Job must have goofed up to deserve all the disasters. There is a learning curve to empathy.

God wants to make me someone who does more than analyze a situation, but who considers the feelings and emotions of situations. That's been a major lesson to me as I've tried to become more effective as a discipler and as someone trying to share my faith in Jesus. How is he trying to connect me emotionally to a friend's job loss, a church member's new baby, the neighbor's kid playing on a championship sports team, or a relative's health problem?

Sure, the message of the cross satisfies the deepest needs of every heart but jumping directly to that issue without engaging the pressing need in that person's life is sometimes self-centered. God has shown me that he will reveal the connection to the Gospel. My job is to love, listen, ask questions, and speak as the Spirit illuminates.

Sensing the guidance of the Spirit will require God developing my emotional self too, in conjunction with the spiritual self. If I've spent a life time shutting down my feelings or dismissing them because they're "untrustworthy," I need to admit that and transfer my whole emotional life to God for his renovation.

I don't want to follow the path of so many who witnessed the ministry of Jesus:

> For this people's heart has become calloused; they hardly hear with their ears, and they have closed their eyes. Otherwise they might see with their eyes, hear with their ears, understand with their hearts and turn, and I would heal them.
>
> MATTHEW 13:15 (NIV)

I want to be someone with a soft heart. I want to be a human being who can sense the Spirit's calling and moving, a person with emotions trained by God's word, and an individual who's emotionally and spiritually mature. I want to be a person who can pull alongside the distressed and discouraged and offer compassion and truth. Then I'll be a useful vessel to my master.

While the movement of the Holy Spirit is very much a sensory, gut level thing, I'm not advocating a no-brain approach. The promptings I sense should be evaluated against the backdrop of truth and the counsel of trusted mature Christian friends. If I think I'm being "led" to have an affair I should rely on the truth of God rather than my emotions. Plus, the Spirit would never lead me into thoughts or behaviors that contradict the Scriptures.

* * * *

Creativity from the Creator

* * * *

Art, music, and dance therapy are all licensed health professional fields in this country, and there's a good reason: researchers have discovered a link between mental health and creative expression. "Artistic self-expression helps people to resolve conflicts and problems, develop interpersonal skills, manage behavior, reduce stress, increase self-esteem and self-awareness, and achieve insight," notes the web site of the American Art Therapy Association, Inc.[7]

This does not mean everyone should become painters and sculptors. That may be counter to the way God made us. Not all of us want to work in oils and acrylics, nor are we all interested in forming globs of clay into a pot or chiseling stone into a heroic figure of history.

But God does want to enlarge my imagination. This is particularly true when it comes to carrying out his commands.

Creativity can be expressed where I am, within who I am, in view of my background and interests. Remember the Bible's beginning paragraphs: "So God created man in his own image, in the image of God he created him; male and female he created them" (Genesis 1:27, NIV).

This verse appears after the fireworks and flash of God's creative outpouring—forming the earth, making day and night, bringing to life ocean critters and land-based animals, plus all the plants and trees. Then he makes man and woman and says we are "made in his own image." We are made in the likeness of a very, very ingenious and inventive person.

Think for a minute about one of Adam's first jobs:

> Now the LORD God had formed out of the ground all the beasts of the field and all the birds of the air. He brought them to the man to see what he would name them; and whatever the man called each living creature, that was its name. So the man gave names to all the livestock, the birds of the air and all the beasts of the field.
>
> GENESIS 2:19–20 (NIV)

Picture that scene! Here's Adam, sifting and categorizing, noticing similarities and discerning distinctions among hundreds and thousands of species. What a highly scientific and imagination-enlarging assignment. God must have supplied Adam with major energy for the task. This creative work was a doozy!

Creativity displays itself in a far-ranging spectrum of abilities and applications. Because of American culture's tendency to lock people's energies into familiar functions done over and over, some of us may not be very aware of our creative gifting.

There's a fellow who lives in my community who owns a tool shop. He sells big commercial lawnmowers and chainsaws and accessories for all kinds of "creative" equipment. Tim Allen would love this man.

What's he best known for? He makes wood sculptures using chainsaws. That's right. He's a chainsaw artist. He's so good at it that my hometown commissioned him to create a man-sized wooden beaver sculpture to serve as the prototype for a whole, umm, uh … what do you call a bunch of beavers? A flock, a herd, a bevy? Anyway, he made the model beaver for our city's big anniversary celebration.

God has an imaginative path for each of us. And it's a passageway that will combine your interests, background, and personality as you carry out a life of service to the Gospel.

Earlier in the book you read about Jim Jinkins. Jim, who is a very creative man, had been serving as a youth minister. But he felt like God's call on him had to do with influencing children's programming with messages informed by biblical love and truth. And he's done that.

Perhaps one of the most creative people of the twentieth century was C.S. Lewis. Among adults he's known as one of the foremost apologists of the Christian faith. But among children he's known for his tales about witches and lions and fauns and centaurs. How many children's hearts have been led to the truth about Jesus Christ through the conveyance of Lewis' imagination? Only in heaven will we know.

There's been a rediscovery of the arts within the

church. Church leaders are discovering and unleashing the imagination of their members through the use of video, drama, and dance. Congregations are singing songs crafted by their own members, not just from the catalogs of Christian music vendors. All of this is designed to bring attention to the source of the creativity. As we're told in Colossians 1:16–17,

> For by him all things were created: things in heaven and on earth, visible and invisible, whether thrones or powers or rulers or authorities; all things were created by him and for him. He is before all things, and in him all things hold together.
>
> COLOSSIANS 1:16–17 (NIV)

Creativity isn't just meant for an art gallery or a Sunday morning service; it should be integrated in all of life.

My friend Dan Bertsos is the director of housing for a state university near us. He and I talk about writing every now and then. He gets to craft a memo here and there which lets his inventive spirit out for a breather. But he's also been a sports coach for his kids. There's an artistic dimension to working with kids and communicating ideas to them in a way that will be meaningful and transfer into action. My friend finds creative satisfaction from that service.

Another friend, Rick Posey, is an architect. You'd think being an architect would be synonymous with far-flung mental navigating. But like any work, you get into habits and patterns that are not so imaginative. Even architects.

One of his spare-time activities is working on his house, which started out as a very simple, single-story family ranch. Rick has added an entire floor to his home and converted a single-car garage into a beautiful living room. We've attended parties in the new space.

"My house is a sculpture," Rick related to me. "Instead of using chisels, I use sledgehammers and drywall."

Sometimes friends or relatives question Rick pouring so much money into a home now worth more than he will ever get out of it. Rick explained, "That's not the way I look at it. The house is a means for me to express my creativity. If I were spending $2000 a year on paints and canvass no one would question that. So I spend that much on my house instead."

My buddy Rob Dant is a very artistic guy. He graduated with a fine arts degree from the Columbus (Ohio) College of Art and Design. But he's not a sculptor, painter, or muralist by trade. He's a residential services specialist who, among other things, designs and maintains the outdoor living space of his clients. "Gardens are about shaping space through form, color, and texture," he notes on his web site. "They should be highly individualized and complement your distinct lifestyle—not just decorate a yard." [8] He's using his God-given creativity in a very creative way.

In addition to this book, I've been working on a number of concurrent projects. There were several columns I wrote about family life for a couple of Christian magazines. I also recently finished a script for an animated cartoon series which exists only in my mind, on my hard drive, and in one printed copy which I read to my daughter Bethany.

I have an interest in kids. I make up dialogue for our cats and dog. I love animated shows. I have a decent sense of humor. Still, I had to stretch a bit to put all this together in a fun, kid-oriented narrative. I felt the

Lord wanted me to share my convictions as a believer through the medium of story. I can't see the end game yet; we'll see what God does with it.

In the process of scriptwriting I've discovered something new about myself—I'm a storyteller. I've been a reporter, telling other people's stories, but through animation script writing I've begun to unlock something else about me. I glory in this, not as an end unto itself, but as one more way God can use me to do things that have eternal value. He's amazing.

Writing this book has been a stretching creative experience. Writing anything more than 2000 words would have seemed way out of reach for me even a couple of years ago. I've written newspaper and magazine stories of 200–2000 words for almost twenty years now. But God was pushing me to stretch out this way. So here we are, almost 60,000 words later.

I've also become, and perhaps this is the topper ... a chalk artist. Well, only around my house, using our sidewalks and driveway as a canvass. Julia does it too. We've drawn just about every cartoon character our kids have imagined over the years, using big colored chalk on the cement around our home.

Many view creative pursuit as beyond their grasp. Fear is the culprit. Creative expression is very personal and intimate. It's letting out in the open thoughts and ideas they've massaged and worked over for years but never risked expressing.

They fear the way people will respond to their creativity. It seems, and I think this may be more of a male thing, a waste of time. Where's the money in this? Such people need to have room in their relationship with God and with a few trusted others where they let the unruly, out-of-the-ordinary side out to play.

Rich Diesslin is a cartoonist. He hasn't made vast sums of money doing this, but he has a web site and he's been published in magazines and has a book of Bible-based cartoons. He's also a technical guy who likes computers and is very analytical. What would my friend be without that creative side? He wouldn't be who God really made him to be. He wouldn't be the guy I know. Just because his creative expression isn't lucrative doesn't mean he shouldn't follow it. Especially as it brings glory to God.

There's a really wrong idea in our society, that I've conformed to as well, that defines value by how much money is attached to a thing. This is not the way God sees it. When he concocted the world, including mankind, he paused at the end of the task and said, "It is good." He didn't put a dollar sign on it and then say, "It is good." The artistic work was intrinsically good apart from any price tag.

• • • •

Unguardedness

• • • •

Exploring creativity has led me, in a backdoor kind of way, into one other region of growth—becoming an unguarded person.

Several years ago I heard a number of people say that I was not very open. What did that mean? I consider myself a very open person. Plus, as a guy, how open should I be? After numerous people said it different ways I understood: I wasn't very revealing about how problems or happy events were touching me; I also didn't share much about my thought processes as I walked through difficulties with the Lord.

I tend to let things hit me—like having a person leave our church for instance—and then let my thoughts and emotions age like a fine wine before serving them up in some orderly, unemotional and, in my view, palatable fashion. This was one example of my guarded style.

God is calling us to be unguarded people, the kind of people who can take the blows of life and still be real and sincere. Even if I'm an effusive, talkative person, what do I really say as I chat on and on? I know very talkative people who tell you little about what's *really* going on.

The thing I'm trying to describe is sometimes referred to as transparency. It's that ability to talk about feelings, emotions, fears and doubts, failures and problems, not worrying about how such revelations make you look in the eyes of others. Such sharing not only helps the sharer but also those who hear because they get a nuts-and-bolts look at walking with Jesus through the realities of life. It's an important aspect of disciple-making.

The Apostle Paul is an interesting case study of unguardedness. Paul is a rough and ready guy at the beginning of the book of Acts. He's a defender of the traditions of his fathers, a religious zealot who thought that arresting and killing Christians was a way to honor God.

Paul was a hard-driving person and, you might assume, not really open. At that time it was mostly about the résumé—circumcised on the eighth day, from the tribe of Benjamin, a Hebrew of Hebrews. His folks had the money or connections or both to send Paul to Jerusalem to learn under Gamaliel, one of the leading rabbis of his day. He was way ahead of his peers, as he explains in Philippians 3. But then something happened—he met Christ in a blinding light on the highway to his next persecution.

Paul's description of his conversion to King Agrippa adds to this picture of a hard driving, hard-hearted person,

> About noon, O king, as I was on the road, I saw a light from heaven, brighter than the sun, blazing around me and my companions. We all fell to the ground, and I heard a voice saying to me in Aramaic, "Saul, Saul, why do you persecute me? It is hard for you to kick against the goads."
>
> ACTS 26:13–14 (NIV)

I don't know about you but I haven't run into any "goads" lately. Good thing. According to the Merriam-Webster's online dictionary, a goad is "a pointed rod used to urge on an animal."[9]

"Kick against the goads" was a Greek proverb, apparently originating with the playwright Euripides. It had to do with fighting against a god.[10] The Lord was telling Paul that striking the church was the same as striking God. Subconsciously Paul was beating his fists against the Rock of Gibraltar, expecting to bring it down with his blows. Tough guy!

But years later we see a transformed, unguarded Paul,

> We have spoken freely to you, Corinthians, and opened wide our hearts to you. We are not withholding our affection from you, but you are withholding yours from us. As a fair exchange—I speak as to my children—open wide your hearts also.
>
> 2 CORINTHIANS 6:11–13 (NIV)

Or look at his first letter to the Thessalonian church,

> As apostles of Christ we could have been a burden to you, but we were gentle among you, like a mother caring for her little children. We loved you so much that we were delighted to share with you not only the gospel of God but our lives as well, because you had become so dear to us.
>
> 1 Thessalonians 2:6b-8 (niv)

God transformed Paul into a person who could express tenderness, love, and caring and still be the same guy who wished that those who pervert the Gospel would emasculate themselves. He was still a sharp, intense man, but someone who was kindhearted and definitely unguarded.

How will God change me? What kind of a person will I be as I obey Jesus' call to this wild ride of altering my life for his sake? Whatever I do, I need to beware satisfaction with the husk I'm living in. Granting carte blanche to the Farmer is the best choice.

Section 4: Grasping the Big Picture

In one sense, mountain climbers have it easy. They can assess the nature of the challenge in front of them by consulting maps and talking to others who've made the ascent to gain a general sense of the terrain. They can fly over the mountain and plan routes carefully.

As a spiritual adventurer, the bigger picture may be more difficult to imagine. But the Bible explains it in great detail. So, for this section, we'll look at three different areas you ought to think about:

- It's about your whole life
- It's about your relationship with God
- It's about spiritual warfare

And while we're at it, let's offer the Lord another prayer: Lord, help me understand what I'm really endeavoring to do; grant me encouragement from this and not a sense of being overwhelmed; teach me how I'll have to rely on You in an even greater way.

It's About Your Whole Life

Jesus is all about cracking open the shell we live in. And the way he does this can seem totally nutty (yes, a pun, forgive me please; I'm glad the Lord does).

There's Peter, sitting in the boat in Matthew 14:22–31. Peter knew plenty about boats. He was a fisherman. He probably used a boat every day. He'd been in a boat thousands of times—in clear weather, sudden storms, choppy waters, hot days, cold days.

Peter also knew a lot about water. He wasn't afraid to get in the water (look at John 21:7). He made his living from the water and he returned to the water after Jesus' death.

But what does Jesus do in Matthew 14? He forces a reassessment of boats and water through a very memorable exchange on the Sea of Galilee. That's when Jesus told Peter and the boys to go ahead without him while he prayed and recovered from the feeding of the 5000.

During the middle of the night the guys saw what they thought was a ghostly figure on the waves and they were scared:

> But Jesus immediately said to them: "Take courage! It is I. Don't be afraid." "Lord, if it's you," Peter replied, "tell me to come to you on the water."
> "Come," he said. Then Peter got down out of the boat, walked on the water and came toward Jesus.
> MATTHEW 14:27–29 (NIV)

With one command, Jesus confronts Peter's conclusions about boats and water. In rough waters you stay in the boat, and the waters had been rough. And if you get out of the boat, you better be ready to get wet. Jesus says, "Go against your instincts about boats and water and come to me."

There's another piece to the story. Matthew writes,

> But when he saw the wind, he was afraid and, beginning to sink, cried out, "Lord, save me!" Immediately Jesus reached out his hand and caught him. "You of little faith," he said, "why did you doubt?"
> MATTHEW 14:30–31 (NIV)

Peter's been scolded as Mr. Foot-in-Mouth by preachers and church leaders through the centuries and he deserves it. But he is so human. Out of all the apostles, he's the one whose character flaws are bared the most in Scripture. You and I and your next door neighbor can relate to him. He was a normal person.

So the wind starts blowing and he's thinking, as I would, *Hey, I should be back in the boat because that's where it's safe* (old point of view), *not out here hydroplan-*

ing with Jesus (new point of view). Then he starts to go for a swim and Jesus rescues him accompanied with the reprimand, "You of little faith; why did you doubt?"

Winds will smack us in the face too. As we skim the waters with Christ, we'll get hit with challenges of "why did you do this; this is insane?" or "how are you planning to support yourself and your family?" or "what a waste of a promising future," whether from within or from family members, colleagues, acquaintances.

We'll get rocked by failures at home, in ministry, and in our personal lives that will make us wonder why we chose to get out of the boat in the first place. We will get soaked as we learn to walk on the water. But one thing for sure, if I keep trying to walk where once I only dog paddled, I won't be the same person for long. And I'll stay on top longer.

• • • •

SOS!

• • • •

What are my "boats"? What are the places, people or things I run to for sure footing when there's trouble in my life, or when I'm questioning what life is about?

If I'm not sure, here's a small exercise. I should think back to a time, or maybe it's something I'm facing right now, when I questioned my value as a person. Perhaps I lost a job, or a relationship went bad or I didn't make the team. What did I think about to steady myself and stop the self-esteem freefall?

For instance, I use maps. Yes, maps. Because maps can take you places that are a good distance from whatever's messing with my joyful mojo. Julia, the kids and I have a record of taking relaxing, rejuvenating and memory-building trips. I reflect on those times with a lot of fondness and our photo albums testify to their value in our family's history.

So, what's the problem? For the most part, there is no problem. It's okay to plan vacations. It's okay to reminisce. God is the God of all comfort, who knows how to comfort us in our time of need. There's a place for those kinds of recollections to help us get through hardships.

When touchstones become fortresses, then I run into trouble. This shows up in my desire to seek out a duplication of some past family experience which translates into map obsession. *Oh, wouldn't this be a cool place to visit and have a lot of fun and absolutely avoid dealing with the issue that's rocking my ego-based joy right this second*, I might subconsciously reason. At that moment, pleasure has become my safe place rather than the Lord.

Here's another confession: I've gained a certain amount of peace and stability from pondering our bank accounts. We've built up a decent retirement fund and, in my moments of personal despair, I'll go online to look at how things are going with the mutual funds. Maybe my freelancing career is in a nosedive but hey, our net worth is doing okay.

This is a sick type of security, and knowing that, I have to report it to the Lord, and reaffirm once more, for the eight millionth time, that he tacked this sin to the cross along with the thousands of others. What is the sin? Anytime I place my hope and peace in something other than God, I'm guilty of breaking numero uno in the big ten list, "You shall have no other gods before me" (Exodus 20:3, NIV).

More than anything or anyone, the Lord God who made the heavens and earth deserves to be my shelter.

The psalmist said it well: "The LORD is my rock, my fortress and my deliverer; my God is my rock, in whom I take refuge" (Psalm 18:2, NIV).

• • • •

Boat Hopping Anyone?

• • • •

When I choose to loosen my grip on my identity as a professional, as a parent, as "the good kid"—however I like to think of myself—then I will find my mind turning to other sources of joy. "Nature abhors a vacuum," French monk François Rabelais wrote.[11] So does my need for security. What I'm saying is this: something has been removed or altered that once gave me a fixed point of security about myself, like my parenting role or a job; the part of me the Bible calls "the flesh" then tries to fill that vacuum with anything but God. This is true for me, even as a believer.

Once I've surrendered my life to the Lord, I may find that, instead of trying to skim the waters, I'm just boat hopping. I'm still in the harbor, leaping from vessel to vessel, rather than skating on top of the deep blue with Christ.

This is good to know at the beginning of trying to follow Christ in a more abandoned way. If I understand my natural drift toward non-God security, I know that I'll need to be prayerful about this. I'll need to share this with trusted brothers in Christ who can check on where my sense of safety is coming from—Jesus or something else.

So, while I'm giving God my career or my status as a parent, why not hand over a few other precious sources of world-based peace:

My stuff. This may be the easiest one of all. Except for that car I've been fixing up in the garage. God can have anything but that. Or my collection of decorative angels. Or the high speed internet connection. Okay, okay, enough already, I want to keep it all!

Psalm 24 speaks to this, "The earth is the Lord's and everything in it; the people and all who live in it" (Psalm 24:1, NIV). My belongings belong to him. Can I let go of them and put them in his hands? It's all going back to him in the end anyway.

Here's one way this has worked out in my life. We have a collection of miniature lighthouses, mostly inherited from my dad. We've also managed to pick up an item here and there—a lighthouse soap dispenser, lighthouse picture frames, and a large ceramic lighthouse. We've put some of these out for public viewing, but we've kept a whole portion of this stuff in our master bathroom for a number of years.

We hold a beach party once a year for our junior high ministry. I decided one year to put the bedroom stuff out for public use. And it's stayed there. I hesitated at first. What if it gets broken? How important is it to God if this stuff gets used by the general public? Not to say I shouldn't have some stuff that's just for me. But the question I faced at the time was this one: could these items be used by God in our efforts to be hospitable?

Our friends, Roger and Lynn Brucker, have always blown me away with their loose hold on possessions, whether it's a car, their pool, books, computers—you name it. We've benefited from the material blessing God's provided them. They have been an example Julia and I have learned from.

My family. That means my spouse, kids and any

other significant people in my life—parents, in-laws, siblings. Remember Jesus' words in Luke 14:26? "If anyone comes to me and does not hate his father and mother, his wife and children, his brothers and sisters—yes, even his own life—he cannot be my disciple" (Luke 14:26, NIV).

Jesus wasn't saying I actually should hate everyone. That contradicts the rest of Scripture. Sacrificial, unconditional love should be the increasing norm in the life of the growing believer. No, what he's saying is, "I come first, ahead of all other people in your life."

Jesus is talking about a heart attitude that's characterized by this decision to say to him, "Here are these relationships and the way I see myself in them. They all belong to you. I want to follow your will in the way I act as a spouse, parent, child, and sibling."

My dreams. I can surrender my talents and abilities and maybe I can even turn over my family and career aspirations. But my dreams? Now wait a minute! Some of those dreams involve career and family. Others involve financial security, retirement, home, etc. Can I put my dreams in God's hands? It's the only logical reaction to his love. And he's really the only person capable of handling them well.

The pointed observation of James says a lot about this attitude:

> Now listen, you who say, "Today or tomorrow we will go to this or that city, spend a year there, carry on business and make money." Why, you do not even know what will happen tomorrow. What is your life? You are a mist that appears for a little while and then vanishes. Instead, you ought to say, "If it is the Lord's will, we will live and do this or that."
>
> JAMES 4:13–15 (NIV)

This is not an anti-planning passage. The problem is what's left out—giving first consideration to what the Lord would want. Plans should be made based on the guidance the Lord gives me.

It's also okay to dream. Paul dreamed of taking the Gospel to Rome. Did he make it? Yes, but not the way he imagined.

Look at Psalm 37:4 for a moment: "Delight yourself in the LORD and he will give you the desires of your heart" (NIV).

As I delight in my relationship with God and the things that are important to him, my heart will begin desiring, and dreaming about, things related to that relationship. But in the end, can I say, "Your dreams, your plans—that's what matter Lord."

My friends. Am I willing to give my friendships to the Lord? Some of my friendships may have lots of history. Putting those relationships in God's hands may be scary. If it's a non-Christian friend then God may want me to bring him into that relationship more. If it's a Christian friend, then God may want me to center my relationship around him more.

When I put friendships in God's hands, he may call on me to intentionally form friendships with people whom I wouldn't naturally be friends. But because of this person's spiritual openness and desire, it makes sense to spend more time with this person, even though:

1.   He may be different from me in small or big ways;

2.   I would not have been friends with this guy in high school, or;

3. I may find this person embarrassing to be around in some situations.

I love these words from a song called "Perception" by Wayne Watson,

> They saw me eatin' at the table with the sinners, tax collectors, the harlots and the thieves. Sometimes I wonder should I be more careful 'bout what people are thinking, what they choose to believe. They saw me talking to that woman at the fountain. I heard 'em whisper, "What's he doing with her?" Guess I can suffer in people's estimations for the transformation of one sinner to occur.[12]

God's in charge of this process. He will bless me as I faithfully pursue his plan for friendship and He will enlarge my ability to love. He will form deep bonds between me and people I never thought I could love. He will bring me into deeper fellowship with himself as I open my heart to friendship with people on the basis of spiritual need rather than what I can get. Start praying today for guidance about how to be a friend and with whom.

My passions. Yep, I've gotta throw in all those avocations of mine—running races, hiking, reading, recreational sports, cycling, watching TV, working in the yard, surfing the Internet. The things that I do in my "spare" time are part of this giving of my total self to God. God wants to use those too.

He wants to use these interests to put me in contact with people who don't know him or to spend time with other believers. He wants to use them to teach me things about himself and myself. He's got plans for these favorite activities of mine.

The Lord will blow my mind as he expands the meaning and purpose of something that was just a pleasant entertainment or a distraction from the humdrum of everyday life. My friend Duane Mueller loves working on cars—his own and other people's. And he turned that over to Christ. I love to hear about the spiritual conversations Duane has, including leading people to faith in Jesus, while working on some guy's carburetor or applying clear coat to a muscle car's paint job.

God wants to fill my activities with divinely ordered meaning so that one day, in his presence, he will be able to say, "Thanks for giving me your interest in rebuilding cars. See these five guys over here? They're here because you did that."

My time. This intersects with many of the topics already discussed—playing a sport or watching TV is how I want to spend "my time." Time, like every other resource, is a stewardship. Moses, that great servant of God, recognized this when he wrote: "Teach us to number our days aright, that we may gain a heart of wisdom" (Psalm 90:12, NIV).

Or, as Job put it, "Man's days are determined; you have decreed the number of his months and have set limits he cannot exceed" (Job 14:5, NIV).

And then one last thought, from King David,

> Show me, O LORD, my life's end and the number of my days; let me know how fleeting is my life. You have made my days a mere handbreadth; the span of my years is as nothing before you. Each man's life is but a breath.
>
> PSALM 37:4–5 (NIV)

God knows the length of each life. Our days are numbered by him. Each day is very literally a gift from our creator and king. Because of this, my first words in the morning should be a prayer that goes something like this: show me Lord how to honor you today with the time you provide.

This point of view rivals our society's view of time—it's my break, my lunchtime, my minute, hour and day. I need to adopt this view instead:

> Be very careful, then, how you live—not as unwise but as wise, making the most of every opportunity, because the days are evil. Therefore do not be foolish, but understand what the Lord's will is.
>
> EPHESIANS 5:15–17 (NIV)

"My" time is not mine to burn. It's a gift God has given me to manage for His sake. So I need to make it my first priority to understand what the Lord's will is, by reading his Word, getting into some deep friendship/fellowship with other Christians, praying and doing service in his name. These are excellent top-drawer choices for how to use the fleeting moments God gives.

•　•　•　•

Dry-Dock the Boats

•　•　•　•

Peter changed because he decided to get out of the boat. He started out brash, big-mouthed, and more concerned about the opinions of others than his Lord. He became a powerful, humble, confident evangelist and pastor. He transitioned into what Jesus called him to be because he set aside what was comfortable and normal for something crazy and exciting—following Jesus! He turned from Shaky (a rough translation of his original name, Simon) to Rocky (*Peter* means "rock").

As I dry-dock the many "boats" in my life, I will begin to change. As I move away from the things or perspectives that have brought me comfort in the past I'll notice a reconstitution of who I am. I'll be satisfied and steadied by a life I would have rejected only months or years before. I'll find myself happier out of the boat than in.

It's About Your Relationship with God

There's a nature preserve near our home. During the first few years in our house the preserve was primitive, well, except for the sound of cars and trucks passing by a couple miles away. Okay, I'll modify—for twenty-first-century suburban America it was primitive.

There were worn paths from past hikers and you could roughly follow a course through the trees, but everything was naturally unkempt: big logs lying all over, plenty of thickets and underbrush, hawthorn trees ready to drop spike bombs, open rocky areas along a creek, perfect for skipping stones and discovering wildlife.

Several years ago our county received a grant from the state of Ohio allowing them to improve the preserve. They put in a couple bridges, erected official-looking signs describing the ecology of the marshes and prairies, and built viewing platforms along the creek. I love all that. I enjoy using that reserve now more than ever.

But it's not enough. So we still go off the path into areas that haven't been prettied up but we love nonetheless.

By putting my family life, my future, my work life, and my comfort before the Lord I have officially jumped off the authorized hiking trail, with lots of neat little bridges traversing streams and gulleys, hand railings on the steep parts and plenty of soft mulch underfoot. Instead my trail will look something more like the one David, Bethany, and I climbed in Honduras—steep and ungainly, no handrails, hairpin switchbacks, slippery, and potentially dangerous. Beautiful to be sure, but wilder and not as safe.

Because of this choice to follow God with greater abandon I'm going to need my spiritual muscle built up each day. Not only will I be climbing uphill, but I'll encounter tricky ledges, uneven footing and the occasional rockslide.

What are the disciplines of a person engaging this book's main question? Stuff you've heard before: read the Bible, pray, seek accountability. I've been doing this hike for more than twenty years and God keeps showing me new things about my climbing gear that I hadn't realized or appreciated.

· · · ·

Scripture: Ready for an Energy Bar?

· · · ·

One of the guys in my small group men's study is Joe Kenney. He devours the Bible like a starving man at an all-you-can-eat buffet. Every time I ask him what he's reading he's pressed on to some new book; he has more questions ("Why in the Old Testament did God order that everyone in Canaan be wiped out?"—Joe asks good questions); and we're talking about what book of the Bible is next for him. Joe gets to work before his early morning shift starts and reads in his car or in the break room till it's time to clock in.

Joe's habit reminds me of David's observation:

> The ordinances of the LORD are sure and altogether righteous. They are more precious than gold, than much pure gold; they are sweeter than honey, than honey from the comb.
>
> PSALM 19:9B-10 (NIV)

Regular, daily consumption of the Word is required. Just like mountain climbers need energy and will hit a wall of exhaustion if they don't, I'll find the same thing happening if I'm not feeding on God's truth *every day*.

I'm a big believer in truth snacking. I've memorized probably forty to fifty Bible verses, either because of a class I've taken or just because I wanted to. I regularly pull up those verses during the day to "snack" on. Sometimes those verses are my only food for the day. Since I've tucked enough of these supernatural energy bars away, I've always got them around, especially in the heat of battle when I don't have time to dig around in the Scripture "fridge."

When Satan is accusing me of being an incompetent bum, I grab a verse like 2 Corinthians 3:5: "Not that we are competent in ourselves to claim anything for ourselves, but our competence comes from God" (NIV).

This verse doesn't excuse me from getting to know

the Bible. Another verse, 2 Timothy 2:15, helps counter that idea: "Do your best to present yourself to God as one approved, a workman who does not need to be ashamed and who correctly handles the word of truth" (2 Timothy 2:15, NIV).

Verses like this remind me that, yes, I should know the Bible, but it's God who makes me successful in serving him, not my own charisma or brainpower. On my own I will go too soft when I should be tougher on myself or others; on my own, I'll be too harsh when I should be more tender and patient.

Even with the energy bars stuck in the backpack of my mind, I still need regular feeding. God revealed that to me while working on this book.

Working on a project like this is a risky venture. There's no guarantee someone will want it. As a writer you wrestle with doubts about the value of what you're saying. You can feel your feet slipping as you begin to wonder, "Why didn't I stick with my more predictable life?"

On one particular day in this literary sojourn I was rolling around on such thoughts like a fawn trying to stand on gravel. I wondered why I'd spent so much time on a project with so little guaranteed return. I quickly forgot all the great things I'd learned about God, myself, and others through this, the points of growth I could count as gain even if the book never found a publisher. I questioned whether I was much of a writer at all.

Then, in the middle of my rockslide, Julia told me she had a meeting at work, which would mean more childcare and less writing time the following day. Julia was only letting me know about a meeting which had been scheduled by others and required her presence. No malice there. But it functioned as that little bit of a shove that caused my tipping psyche to look over the cliff's edge. I knew I was in trouble.

While Julia headed for the bathtub for her nightly relaxation time, I made my way down the stairs to the living room, where several Bibles were. I didn't know what to read, but I knew I needed to attach myself to something firm. So I read through the Psalms and slowly felt myself not sliding anymore. Julia came downstairs after her bath and asked if I was okay. My answer? "I just knew I needed to get my head straight; I'm doing better now."

Right there I was in total agreement with David as he discussed the truths of God: "By them is your servant warned; in keeping them there is great reward" (Psalm 19:11, NIV).

Scripture keeps us from harm, warning us against lies and half-truths that will hurt us and others, mainly by revealing what the real picture is, i.e., yes, my circumstances stink right now, but the Bible says God is still in charge and he can creatively cause good to happen from this if I'll hang on and wait (Romans 8:28). Scripture also rewards those who consider it and act upon its declarations about God, his promises, his Son and whom we are if we've asked Jesus to be our savior.

If you're realizing you need to answer God's command to alter your life for Jesus' sake, then get into a small group Bible study fast. That is, if you're not in one already. Get into a study that requires weekly commitment to the Bible. Also, find a time every day (morning, lunchtime, evening or bedtime) when you can read the Bible and reflect on what it says. You'll need a time when you can turn it over in your mind and think about it. If you find yourself skimming over lightly because you're in a rush, then think about another time. Beware reading the Bible too late at night—heavy eyelids are a constant enemy at that time of day. I know that all too well.

Julia reads at night before bed. That's when she relaxes and reflects. It works for her. I have read at bedtime, but I've also gained from a morning reading time. I have to adjust based on what's going on in life.

Get into a Scripture memorization program. For some people, memorizing is very difficult. However, that doesn't mean I shouldn't try. It just means I will need to adjust my expectations of how fast I'll retain Scripture. Julia has a hard time holding on to memory verses, but she's trying just the same. I'm encouraged by her efforts, which are much more an act of faith than memorizing has ever been for me.

I may need to get inventive with memory refreshers. Some people stick the verse of the week on the fridge or write it on a dry erase message board. I created a little contraption once, screwing together two medium-sized paper clamps which I clipped to my rearview mirror. Then I stuck my three by five card in there with that week's verse. I was reminded of that verse every time I looked at the rearview mirror and I'd recite it in my head. What else was I doing during drive time anyway? I might as well make car time productive for God.

The greatest way to hold God's truth is to use it. So, while I'm committing a new verse to my personal database, I usually ask the Lord to give me chances to use that truth in real life—a situation where I need to remember that identity truth from Romans 8:1; a ministry opportunity where I can exhort someone to forgive based on Ephesians 4:31–32.

. . . .

Prayer: Muscle-Building Time

. . . .

I view my prayer time from a number of perspectives—a time to worship the Lord; to acknowledge my moral failures and confirm that I need his grace; to reflect on what God's doing in my life; to discuss the significant relationships in my life; to ask for chances to share my faith and for the courage and clarity to do it well; to seek his intervention in the lives of others; and to battle the spiritual enemy.

Prayer is my daily workout with God. It's a time to get real with him, to listen to his spirit, to get his direction about personal matters, including the way I'm looking at myself. I seek out his counsel and power for character change, get centered on his will and renew my relationship with him.

Unless I go into the cosmic workout room in the morning, I'm spiritually winded before lunch. I just don't have the patience for the growth process or the mindset for what he's doing to keep going. Prayer time is power up time.

I usually get about a half hour of prayer a day. This may seem quite doable or it may sound like climbing Mt. Everest. Don't sweat it. God will meet you where you're at. Aim at something that will be a push for you—say five minutes with the Lord three days a week. Too tepid? If you think God wants you to pray ten minutes a day five days a week then go for it. He's the one leading the process.

Approach your prayer goal like you would an exercise goal. Get consistent at that level before aiming higher. Of course, this isn't competition; it's about developing passion for your relationship with Christ.

Ask your spouse, a close Christian friend, or your kids to hold you accountable about how you're doing with prayer. Your children may end up being your best accountability partners, plus it lets them know they have an important role in how you're doing spiritually.

As I think about this area, I'm reminded of Jesus and the familiar verses about how he pulled away from the crowd to spend time with the Father. This is a quick listing:

> • Immediately Jesus made the disciples get into the boat and go on ahead of him to the other side, while he dismissed the crowd. After he had dismissed them, he went up on a mountainside by himself to pray.
>
> MATTHEW 14:22–23 (NIV)

> • One day Jesus was praying in a certain place. When he finished, one of his disciples said to him, "Lord, teach us to pray, just as John taught his disciples."
>
> LUKE 11:1 (NIV)

> • But Jesus often withdrew to lonely places and prayed.
>
> LUKE 5:17 (NIV)

> • Very early in the morning, while it was still dark, Jesus got up, left the house and went off to a solitary place, where he prayed.
>
> MARK 1:35 (NIV)

The point is simple: to live the counter cultural life he was called to live, Jesus knew he had to have regular, heartfelt, transparent time with the Father. And so away he went, up to a mountainside or into the Garden of Gethsemane.

As much as Jesus' example is instructive, I find two commands he gave his disciples really key. The first is found in Matthew 6:9–10. Yes, it's the first half of Jesus' celestial communication schematic i.e. the Lord's Prayer. Here's what it says: "This, then, is how you should pray: 'Our Father in heaven, hallowed be your name, your kingdom come, your will be done on earth as it is in heaven' (Matthew 6:8–10, NIV).

The whole front end of this prayer is about the transfer of God's kingdom to earth. And how will that be accomplished? Okay, not in a final way till Jesus returns to rule, but until then it happens through us, his people and representatives in the world. The entire beginning of this famous prototype prayer is about God making us into heavenly people on earth, rather than earthly people with tickets punched for heaven.

Then there's this verse out of Luke, spoken to Jesus' disciples hours before his arrest. These guys were having a hard time staying awake. Given the hour of the morning, I may have been in the same condition. But I think if these guys really understood what was about to happen they could not have slumbered. So Jesus commands them, "Why are you sleeping? Get up and pray so that you will not fall into temptation" (Luke 22:46, NIV).

What was the temptation? To be focused on their own comfort and need at a time of great danger. Today, the temptations are no different. Woe to me if I wander into my day spiritually aloof to the war I'm in the middle of, a war in which I'm a principal player and the enemy knows that.

If he can distract or discourage us from pursuing

our calling, Satan will keep us from maturing into a heavenly marine corps capable of doing much damage to his kingdom.

As a believer called to maturity, I must get serious about carving out time to pray. My life and the lives of others really do depend on it.

• • • •

Fellowship: Workout Friends

• • • •

I also need the input of other believers. I need guys who can ask questions about my relationship with Jesus, my wife, and my kids; what God is showing me about character change; who I'm trying to reach out to; how discipleship is going. I need some guys who know how to encourage, exhort, correct, disagree, and pose new points of view.

Solomon got it right when he noted in Proverbs 27:6, "Wounds from a friend can be trusted, but an enemy multiplies kisses" (NIV).

I need other Christians who can wound me—tell me the truth when I may not want to hear it—rather than a bunch of people who will compliment me one hundred percent of the time. Or even worse, be so concerned about keeping peace they don't ask a question or raise an observation which might get me riled up a bit.

How can you tell if you have this? First of all, do you have several people in your life whose lives are centered on their relationship with Jesus? Second, do they ask you how things are going with God? Do they know enough about you to ask about persistent sin issues—your proneness to resolve depression with spending, your tendency to justify unforgiveness, your critical spirit? And do they have the green light to ask those questions? And do they do that?

There needs to be balance, of course, but the best friends know how to parse out the hard news in a kind way. "Speak the truth in love" is God's plan for healthy Christian community and spiritual fullness (Ephesians 4:15).

It's too easy to be swayed by the world's arguments about what kind of person I ought to be: distant and not there emotionally for my family; an entertainment freak constantly seeking the next opportunity for good times and relaxation; or a gadget lover always looking to buy the next high tech toy to make my life temporarily more interesting.

I need Christian friends who will call me on the carpet, who will question my motives, who will ask not just the first question, but then the second, third, and fourth question about why I want to do something or why I acted this way. I need brothers or sisters who will listen as I talk about my life and what I see God trying to do. I need people who will encourage me to follow God in deeper and higher ways.

I need my spouse in this shaping process. I should be relying on my better half for support, for a listening ear, for challenging comments and questions, for prayer, all to help me toward maturity in Christ.

I think about marriage when I read Solomon's statement in the book of Ecclesiastes:

> Also, if two lie down together, they will keep warm.
> But how can one keep warm alone? Though one
> may be overpowered, two can defend themselves. A
> cord of three strands is not quickly broken.
>
> ECCLESIASTES 4:11–12 (NIV)

Our friend Roger read this passage at our wedding. Jesus is the third strand to make a strong cord. But my spouse should be one person I can count on to cover my back, no matter what. And I will need her support, and she will need mine, as we move forward in this adventure of hiking to the summit in Christ.

It's About Spiritual Warfare

The forces may be invisible, but we are at war. We switched sides in the war the minute we accepted Christ as our savior. We were automatically enlisted in God's army the instant we made that choice.

Don't be frightened. The enemy, while smart and experienced, is facing a power which will ultimately defeat him. As Jesus says: "I will build my church, and the gates of Hades will not overcome it" (Matthew 16:18, NIV).

It's an odd phrase, but imagine the army of God charging the gates of hell and overcoming Satan's stronghold. The church, for all its flaws and problems, will not be overcome by Satan's kingdom or held back from conquering.

Until that promised victory, we are in a battle. But it's not a battle as we often see it—big machines firing loud guns and soldiers wearing body armor. Paul describes it this way:

> For though we live in the world, we do not wage war as the world does. The weapons we fight with are not the weapons of the world. On the contrary, they have divine power to demolish strongholds. We demolish arguments and every pretension that sets itself up against the knowledge of God, and we take captive every thought to make it obedient to Christ.
>
> 2 Corinthians 10:3–5 (niv)

The battlefield is my mind and the minds of those in my world. What are the weapons?

Words, ideas, and beliefs. Not just any words or ideas, however, but a verbal armory that has the ability to "demolish arguments and every pretension that sets itself up against the knowledge of God" (2 Corinthians 10:5, niv). There's only one source for those kinds of ideas: the Bible.

As well as I might be able to reason with someone about the existence of God or the dependability of the New Testament manuscripts, nothing possesses the impressive battering-ram power of God's truth.

The Word of God is living and active, according to Hebrews 4:12 (niv). *Active* is synonymous with energetic, powerful and effectual. "Sharper than any double-edged sword, [the Word] penetrates even to dividing soul and spirit, joints and marrow; it judges the thoughts and attitudes of the heart," the rest of the verse states.

Ephesians six inventories a Christian soldier's equipment, most of it defensive. But in the middle of the list is one of the main offensive weapons—the sword of the Spirit, which is the Word of God. The other offensive weapon? Prayer!

There are Christians who know little about spiritual warfare. That's because they've settled for duty in the rear. Or worse, they're AWOL. They've settled for the values of the world. Satan knows he has nothing to fear from such people. But the moment I say to God, "Here is my life" I get Satan's attention.

The devil takes notice of a Christian laying everything before his King because such a person can travel quickly in the spiritual realm that Satan rules. When someone gives Jesus her current lifestyle and priorities she's doing more than responding to her loving savior, she is also serving notice that she's ready for battle.

Satan takes note of a person who will bend, fold and organize her life to serve those at home, church and in the community. Satan knows the power of such a person and he will do whatever he can to derail the growth process in her life.

Because of this we ought to take note of the last part of 2 Corinthians 10:5: "We take captive every thought to make it obedient to Christ" (NIV). In this chapter I will discuss normal battlefield thoughts we must "take captive" and replace with the truth of God.

Following God can get intense. A believer must be convinced there's life beyond this existence and that God's evaluation in the next life matters more than the evaluation of any other person in this one. Satan will take me to the wall on this issue as I give to God the things which make up my identity and sustain my comfort. Satan's goal is to keep my mind off the eternal rewards that make this adventure worth the pain.

For instance, I have to be careful looking at the "Where Are They Now" section of my alma mater's alumni magazine. I start out looking for names I know, then I slip into comparing graduation dates and the title a person has, then I begin to wonder if I could do that job or if I've *forever squandered* the option of doing the work described.

Satan takes what began as innocent curiosity and uses it as the basis for an assault on my choices. I've learned I need to pray before I look at such things, asking God to help me see the record of others' accomplishments through his eyes and not get into unhealthy comparing. If I don't prepare my mind this way I open myself to trouble.

It's times like these when I turn to 2 Corinthians 4,

> Therefore we do not lose heart. Though outwardly we are wasting away, yet inwardly we are being renewed day by day. For our light and momentary troubles are achieving for us an eternal glory that far outweighs them all. So we fix our eyes not on what is seen, but on what is unseen. For what is seen is temporary, but what is unseen is eternal.
>
> 2 CORINTHIANS 4:16–18 (NIV)

Doing the Lord's bidding will bring joy, peace, and purpose this world can't match. Jesus promised that (John 14:27, 16:33). But it will also take me into places and situations that are most decidedly difficult and in some cases extremely hard. And that's where the devil will tempt me to focus on how good it could be rather than how great it will be.

There's a guy named Buck who kept his eyes squarely on the eternal, even though he possessed the brainpower and charisma to live large in the here and now. He put it all on the line, including his career and his family. He was a computer wizard, an insightful teacher, a fun-loving and sometimes reckless daredevil, a tender-hearted dad and husband, a lover of people and messenger of God's grace.

But we won't hear any recent quotes from Buck in this book. He died from injuries received in an accident in Russia. He had lived there a number of years with his wife Amy and two daughters and had won young Russians to faith in Christ. He was intent, with the help of a team of believers, to grow indigenous communities of Christians who could reach their society for the Lord.

Buck had his eyes on the big picture, and that's what drove him. That is what should drive us as well. We need to return to the big picture when the devil is telling us this path we're on is a criminal misuse of time and talent.

In those moments I try to recall 1 Corinthians 4,

> So then, men ought to regard us as servants of Christ and as those entrusted with the secret things of God. Now it is required that those who have been given a trust must prove faithful. I care very little if I am judged by you or by any human court; indeed, I do not even judge myself. My conscience is clear, but that does not make me innocent. It is the Lord who judges me.
>
> 1 CORINTHIANS 4:1–4 (NIV)

God may allow Satan to sift me on this matter. My decision to give up a high paying job may have been accompanied by a high adrenaline rush of excitement. The vision of seeing myself used in the lives of others buoyed my spirit, and the first days, weeks and months of this adventure seemed effortless.

But now I'm into year three of this journey and the thrill is gone. I'm huffing my way through the middle miles of a very long spiritual road race. I'm beginning to read Job and understand his questions. Psalm 10:1 is committed to memory: "Why, O LORD, do you stand far off? Why do you hide yourself in times of trouble?" (NIV).

I look at peers who've stuck with the grind but I'm the one feeling pulverized. To be honest, those poor souls committed to worldly achievement seem, well, it's hard to admit but, yes, they seem happy!

At that moment I have an important question to ask: was this really an eternal values choice? If I can say "yes" then Satan has lost this round. If I can say, "This has never been about how much money I make or my title, but wanting God to use me," then I've passed an important test. I'm another step closer to the goal.

• • • •

The Competency Question

• • • •

Competency is another area where I come under attack. This is my Achilles' heel. I hate to feel ignorant, and nothing has put this to the test more than going off trail with Jesus.

By competent, I mean this: you know what you're doing. You're an expert at what you do, whether you're a full-time parent, accountant, police officer, or school volunteer. You're proficient at what you do. You speak the language of those around you. You've become a kind of Yoda to those who are less experienced and knowledgeable.

When a person makes a decision to alter his lifestyle, even though nothing has changed about his knowledge level or skill, his sense of competence will come under fire. He may hear it from peers. He may think about it himself.

I'm thinking right now about a scene from *Jerry Maguire,* after Jerry has submitted his mission statement about the way sports agents should work. He's urging a commitment to ethics and caring about people. The company fires him.

Jerry sees his old girlfriend, a fellow sports agent, at a football game shortly after his humiliation. As they pass each other she plants the right thumb and forefinger combo in the shape of an *L* on her forehead—the big *L* for "Loser."

The moral of the story: Jerry is not the loser. He's the winner. He hadn't lost any of his professional competence, but has decided to stand for something other than money and big egos. Of course we know he's the winner because his only client, an undersized prima donna wide receiver, lands a mega-million dollar contract at the end of the film. Hey, at least Hollywood got part of the point.

In the midst of warfare over competency stands Satan, tossing little incendiary thoughts—"How come your former good buddy and co-worker hasn't called you about that fantasy football league you're both in?"; "Why haven't you heard from that company that wanted to hire you as a consultant?"; "Why was your supervisor making negative comments during that last performance review?"; "Why hasn't Susan from the club been in touch since you decided to help out more with the youth ministry?"

I've come to see this bombardment of gloom as strangely confirming of my life-altering decision. Satan takes no interest in the person who's happily pursuing this world's path. But he will fire the big guns at the competence of someone who's setting their eyes on heavenly things in the middle of this world. Getting barraged is sort of a backdoor compliment.

I will pray for relief during such attacks and instead of blocking the assault, God will often remind me of truths like 2 Corinthians 12:9–10. He's calling me to decide, over and against my feelings, that although I may be a loser in the world's eyes, that even though I have problems and flaws, it's okay. Actually it's better than okay, it's great, because he can do amazing things through a weak guy like me.

As I affirm God's desire and ability to work through my soft spots, God releases his power in me and through me, and the momentum of the battle changes, usually immediately, sometimes over minutes or even hours.

Another passage written to the Corinthian church bolsters this position:

Where is the wise man? Where is the scholar? Where is the philosopher of this age? Has not God made foolish the wisdom of the world? For since in the wisdom of God the world through its wisdom did not know him, God was pleased through the foolishness of what was preached to save those who believe. Jews demand miraculous signs and Greeks look for wisdom, but we preach Christ crucified: a stumbling block to Jews and foolishness to Gentiles, but to those whom God has called, both Jews and Greeks, Christ the power of God and the wisdom of God. *For the foolishness of God is wiser than man's wisdom, and the weakness of God is stronger than man's strength.*

1 CORINTHIANS 1:20–25 (NIV, EMPHASIS ADDED)

I prefer to be the wise man, the scholar or the philosopher of this age. Being in God's infantry will mean moments of looking like a fool or incompetent or a pushover. I need to know this now. But being a fool for God is better by an exponent of one hundred than being a great person of this age.

• • • •

War at Home

• • • •

Satan will attack on the family front. The expectations of people who love us can be a powerful force in shaping the way we look at ourselves. Do my parents expect me to work a sixty hour work week, make six figures, own a beautiful home, and have two expensive cars? Being in God's infantry will run me smack dab into their expectations and disappointment.

I need to commit myself to loving them, explaining why I'm doing what I'm doing, while not letting Satan bait me into a defensive or argumentative position. I need to be able to tell them, calmly and prayerfully, I've decided to work part time so I can be more available to family and church. Or that I passed up some big promotion because it would take me out of fellowship. When they suggest maybe I should go to seminary, I should kindly respond that it won't be necessary, I like the career I'm in.

As parents see me give up a six-figure income for a five-figure alternative, or for no income at all, they will wonder if I'm doing what's best. I have to remember, Mom and Dad are speaking from their hearts. If they didn't care about me they'd let it go without a word.

On the other hand, my parents may see my vocational transition as a personal slap in the face. Satan will use their disapproval like a howitzer, blasting away at my confidence in God's leading. At that moment I have to recall God's truth that I'm of immense value to my big daddy. He loved me so much he stepped out of heaven into this crazy existence so he could give me the best. Therefore, I need not be afraid of how Mom and Dad may look at me.

Our parents raised us and continue to have an important role in our lives. We should thank God for them, even as they question our judgment and maybe even our sanity. As the author of Hebrews notes: "Our fathers disciplined us for a little while as they thought best; but God disciplines us for our good, that we may share in his holiness" (Hebrews 12:10, NIV).

Mom and Dad directed us as they thought best. Thank the Lord for that. But now, God is challenging us in even higher and better ways. This verse is a powerful weapon for countering the verbal grenades of Satan regarding the opinions of our parents.

As God's warriors we should think of ourselves as under another's command, not the command of society, teachers, supervisors, or even parents. We're under the authority of God. And we have an important job: keepers of the secret things of God. We should make ourselves available to God to get that information out and defend it. The mysterious story of God entering our world as a below-the-poverty-line baby in the middle of nowhere, paying for our sins with his own sinless life, and coming back to life to prove the victory over death—that has been placed in our keeping.

Our lives and speech should reflect the truth of this mystifying but very true set of events. We need to soldier the resources necessary for us to reveal this secret in the spheres of influence where we live and work. We do have a great adversary, who will do what he can to divert us, discourage us, and hamstring us from accomplishing this mission.

Let's close this chapter considering one last Scripture, from 1 John 4, "You, dear children, are from God and have overcome [false spirits], because the one who is in you is greater than the one who is in the world" (1 John 4:4, NIV).

If there's one verse I should definitely, unequivocally, absolutely memorize out of this chapter, this is it. My King is the King. And he's alive in me. I should obey his calling through all of life and go where he tells me to go.

Section 5: One Last Push

Any major achievement will sap you of strength, energy, and courage. Sometimes we need a reminder that it's worth it, and we need to keep on going. I started running a couple years ago and discovered one of the best strategies is going with a friend. There's nothing like mutual encouragement to keep on going.

In this final chapter, which is based on the story of Naomi in the book of Ruth, I encourage you to keep after this goal of giving your work life, your family life, your identity, and your whole self to God and becoming the person he wants you to be. Naomi's story is inspiring. But things begin on a down note. Let's check it out.

There's Hope

Someone reading these pages may think, *All this sounds great but I'll never get there; I'll never be all that God designed me to be.* No one will. Putting my life in the hands of Christ is the beginning of something God will have to complete.

But this person's thoughts may run deeper. *Of course God must complete the project, but I'm not even sure about the process.* He may look at himself and the choices he's made so far and conclude, *I've messed things up too much; I'm too set in my ways; the die is cast.*

In fact, he may even be a little discouraged as he's read this book. Some hurts run deep. Some disappointments can appear too great to overcome. *How can God ever reach into my life in a way that will make me different than what I am today? He can't.*

With God, we should never say can't. Just ask Naomi.

Naomi may not be familiar but perhaps you've heard of Ruth. Sandwiched between Judges and 1 Samuel in the Old Testament, it's an easy story to overlook. Little old Ruth, only four chapters long, can get lost in the shuffle between the stories of Gideon, Samson, and one of the most beloved of all Sunday school characters, King David. Ahh, but Naomi's story has a direct link to the famed giant killer. Let's see how.

The book of Ruth really should be titled Naomi, because it's her story more than anyone else's. Ruth, while a vital and important character, is merely playing a role in the larger plan of God for the salvation of humanity (that's all!) while also being used by God to retrieve Naomi from a life of bitter despair. God is the great pursuer and wooer, and he knew exactly the best way to pursue and woo Naomi.

Naomi escaped Israel with her husband and two sons during a distressing famine. They moved to the neighboring land of Moab. While there Naomi's sons married Moabite women, one of them the famous Ruth. But tragedy struck. Not only did Naomi lose her husband, but her two sons died as well.

As agonizing as this situation might be for any woman in any culture during any time, it carried a double whammy for Naomi. Without a husband or son she was destitute. There was no opportunity for training or obtaining gainful employment. It looked like Naomi would be relegated to the life of a beggar.

So we meet Naomi coming home to Israel, after attempting to shoo her two daughters-in-law back home. But faithful Ruth stuck with her mother-in-law. It couldn't have been an easy trip.

As soon as Naomi enters her old hometown of Bethlehem (cue the narrative foreshadowing music:

dum-dum-duh … duh!) people are buzzing about her return. "Is that Naomi? Sure looks like Naomi. Wow, I think that's Naomi." That Naomi's return would cause such a tumult may indicate Bethlehem wasn't a real happening place. What was Naomi's response to all the attention?

> When they arrived in Bethlehem, the whole town was stirred because of them, and the women exclaimed, "Can this be Naomi?"
> "Don't call me Naomi," she told them. "Call me Mara, because the Almighty has made my life very bitter. I went away full, but the LORD has brought me back empty. Why call me Naomi? The LORD has afflicted me; the Almighty has brought misfortune upon me."
>
> RUTH 1:19–21 (NIV)

Why the name change? I've never asked anyone to stop calling me "Clem" although I've asked people to stop calling me variations on my name, offered by alleged friends over the years.

The request for a name change indicates the depths of Naomi's hopelessness. Her given name, *Naomi*, means "pleasant" in Hebrew while the name she requested, *Mara*, means, yes that's right, "bitter." Oh the cruel ironies! I'm sure even hearing her own name at this point was a kind of strange, distorted torture, hauling up memories of better times when she really believed her name was a harbinger of good from God.

As the story progresses, Naomi agrees to let Ruth go out to the farmers' fields around town to glean the leavings from the harvest. Leaving something for the poor, rather than picking up every single last grain of wheat, was commanded by God in Leviticus 19:9–10 and 23:22.

Ruth ended up gleaning in the fields of a man named Boaz, who was a distant relative of Naomi's. Naomi had no knowledge of this and had not directed Ruth to go there. Ruth just ended up there by divine intervention.

When Boaz notices the young woman picking up stray bits of food from his fields and asks about her, his foreman comments,

> She is the Moabite who came back from Moab with Naomi. She said, "Please let me glean and gather among the sheaves behind the harvesters." She went into the field and has worked steadily from morning till now, except for a short rest in the shelter.
>
> RUTH 2:6B-7 (NIV)

Boaz decides to speak with Ruth himself.

> "My daughter, listen to me. Don't go and glean in another field and don't go away from here. Stay here with my servant girls. Watch the field where the men are harvesting, and follow along after the girls. I have told the men not to touch you. And whenever you are thirsty, go and get a drink from the water jars the men have filled."
> At this, she bowed down with her face to the ground. She exclaimed, "Why have I found such favor in your eyes that you notice me—a foreigner?"
> Boaz replied, "I've been told all about what you have done for your mother-in-law since the death of your husband—how you left your father and mother and your homeland and came to live with a people you did not know before. May the lord repay you for what you have done. May you be richly rewarded by

the lord, the God of Israel, under whose wings you have come to take refuge."

Ruth 2:8–12 (niv)

Boaz turns out to be a man of noble character, the kind of man I'd want my own daughter to marry someday. He makes a decision to open his fields to Ruth and to make sure she's safe when she works there. He asks for nothing in return. He's simply responding to the character and faithfulness of Ruth in kind.

When Ruth reports the news to Naomi, she has a much different response than when she first crossed Bethlehem city limits. Noticing the bushels of food, she asks Ruth where she had worked. Ruth explained she had been in the fields of Boaz,

> "The lord bless him!" Naomi said to her daughter-in-law. "He has not stopped showing his kindness to the living and the dead." She added, "That man is our close relative; he is one of our kinsman-redeemers."

Ruth 2:20 (niv)

Long story short: Boaz was a guy who could restore to Naomi the property of her late husband. But this isn't just about property rights or financial security. This event is meaningful because it takes Naomi back to her beliefs and feelings about God. "He (Yahweh) has not stopped showing his kindness to the living and the dead" (Ruth 2:20, niv). God had not forgotten her.

God never forgets us (see Psalm 139:2–3), but I may not have been in the right posture to receive the blessings he had in mind. The Lord may bring difficulties, hardships, and a real breaking of my expectations before he can ladle on his goodness. He may allow our dreams to shatter so that we might say, from the heart, "What do you want me to do?"

Reflecting on Naomi's story, Larry Crabb observed, "Until we know how close we come to giving up on God, we'll known little of what it means to give ourselves fully to God."[13]

And God intended to pour a lot of goodness into Naomi's life, as the rest of the story portrays.

Boaz is able to purchase back the land that belonged to Naomi's husband. And more than that, he marries Ruth and they have a child, thereby extending the family name in that culture. The closing lines of the book say it all:

> The women said to Naomi: "Praise be to the LORD, who this day has not left you without a kinsman-redeemer. May he become famous throughout Israel! He will renew your life and sustain you in your old age. For your daughter-in-law, who loves you and who is better to you than seven sons, has given him birth." Then Naomi took the child, laid him in her lap and cared for him. The women living there said, "Naomi has a son." And they named him Obed. He was the father of Jesse, the father of David.
>
> RUTH 4:14–17 (NIV)

Isn't that amazing? Look at that last quote for a moment: "Naomi has a son." This is not a typographical mistake. The neighbor ladies did not say, "Naomi has a grandson," but instead "Naomi has a son." God had remembered Naomi and given her a child who would bless her, but who would also be used in God's plan to bless the whole world. And he did so using the oddest set of twists and curves.

I may be in a spot where I wonder what God can

do. Perhaps I remember a time in my life when I was more "sold out" for God but that seems like a dusty memory. There was a time when I wanted a rich life—not riches but richness. How did I arrive at thinking that a comfortable lifestyle and dependable schedule were a fulfillment of John 10:10? Remember that verse? "I have come that they may have life, and have it to the full." (John 10:10, NIV)

He can take me and make me something better than I ever imagined—if I give him the chance. Adopting God's view and putting my lifestyle and current circumstances in his hands today is the only reasonable answer. Right now. I shouldn't wait. The most exciting days of my life for Jesus are just ahead.

Study Guide: Questions for Reflection

. . . .

Section 1: Imagine a Different Life
Why Am I Thinking about This?

. . . .

1. What are your values? Write them down. Not sure? Ask God to reveal them to you. Maybe this will help unlock things. Write down the kind of life you hope your kids will have. This will show you quite a bit about your values.

2. Who helped shape your values: Mom, Dad, coach, pastor, etc.? What about that person affected the way you look at life? How does their influence square with God's values?

3. What circumstances are causing you to re-evaluate your life? What are you realizing about yourself, God, and others?

4. What do you fear about making a change in your life? What excites you about this possibility? What's the worst thing that could happen? What's the best?

• • • •

Who Am I Anyway?

• • • •

1. How do you tend to view your spiritual life? Be honest here—is it boring? Or comfortable? Have you ever thought of your faith as exciting or thrilling?

2. Have you ever had an experience which opened your spiritual eyes in a new way? What was it? Maybe you read a book that made the lights go on, or some event expanded your vision. What did you "see" in a new way?

3. When have you felt the best about yourself? Was it triggered by an achievement, a comment from someone important, the purchase of something you really wanted? When you helped someone in trouble? What would it take to develop God-based self-esteem?

4. Have you ever felt enslaved to other's opinions? For example, you would like to do something else with your life, but your fear of letting significant people down holds you back. How would knowing

and beginning to apply your identity as God's child change this situation?

· · · ·

What Will It Cost Me?

· · · ·

1. What are the costs you may face as you consider making a lifestyle change?

2. If you could rely on your spouse to pull more of the income load, would you consider stepping back in your career and make less money?

3. Could you give God more of your time? Could you say to him right now, "God, here's all the time I spend watching TV, surfing the Web, reading books, playing sports; do with it what you want." Do you find it difficult making this kind of open-ended offer to God? Why?

· · · ·

How Will I Get There?

· · · ·

1. What do you think your mission is?

2. There are a number of options when considering life alteration: arranging childcare to work/volunteer outside the home, working at a job primarily for the relationships, working at a job that permits extra free time but less pay, or giving up work altogether or to a significant degree. Do any of these strike a chord? What other possibilities might there be?

3. Have you ever felt God's pull or direction in a very clear way? How have you felt God's nudging? What needs to happen in your life so you can sense God's leading?

• • • •

Section 2: Case Studies
Paul: The Leather Craftsman

• • • •

1. Have you ever thought about Paul working more as a leather craftsman than an apostle? How do you think Paul did it? How does this change your perception of Paul?

2. Does your current life situation permit you to "seek the good of many, so that they may be saved"? Is this a valid way of evaluating your life?

3. How do you view your career? How does it compare with the way Paul looked at his main job of being a leather worker?

4. What do you think about Paul's assessment of his life before knowing Christ? How would you assess your life before knowing Christ? After?

• • • •

Phil Wong: Following the Past into the Present

• • • •

1. Phil Wong is doing quite divergent things with his work life: bio-medical engineering and cross-cultural publishing. What are the yearnings of your spirit with regard to paid or unpaid work? Do they seem at odds from one another?

2. Phil comments on his life, "As I look back at that awful experience [of racism], I can see how good came out of it in what God wants me to do." How

might God be drawing you to something from your past to show you his way in the future?

3. He also said, "The cash flow has been negative, which is uncomfortable, but I feel like I'm where God wants me to be." How would you deal with that situation?

• • • •

Donna Jordan-Mitchell: A Better Epitaph

• • • •

1. Donna Jordan imagined how her epitaph might read and this convinced her to make a change in her life. How would your epitaph read right now? Is that what you want it to say?

2. Donna talked about "green lights" which confirmed the direction she was going. What kind of green lights is God providing as you think about changing your life?

3. Donna's husband Steve has inspired her to follow God in a more abandoned way. Who in your life influences you like that?

• • • •

Tim Norman: Different Soil, More Fruit

• • • •

1. Even though Tim was doing "good work" at West Virginia University, he sensed there was more. Is that where you're at? What "more" might you be seeking?

2. Tim and Robin found it hard to get straight answers from friends, ministers and others about the path they should take. What kind of input are you getting? Do you have someone who knows you well enough to zero in on passions, gifts, and the Lord's leading in your life?

3. Tim comments, "If you stay in the safe place and don't give [God] a chance to show you he's in charge, you shut down a growth path." What do you think Tim is saying? How might it apply to you?

• • • •

Jim Jinkins: From Youth Pastor to Animator

• • • •

1. Jim Jinkins and David Campbell have had a level of success that many could only dream of. Yet they jumped out of those apparently "perfect" careers to pursue God's calling. What would cause you to jump out of your current "perfect" situation to do what God wanted you to?

2. Jim explains there are no guarantees with the business plan for Cartoon Pizza. How would you deal with that uncertainty? How could it be an opportunity for spiritual growth?

3. Reflect on Jim's statement, "This message that God leads and cares for me keeps me pushing and trying things, meeting people and thinking. You never know how things will connect." This suggests an active, rather than a passive, approach to discover-

ing God's will. What do you think about that? How does that square with Scripture?

• • • •

Dean Ridings: Good Works vs. "Good" Money

• • • •

1. At the cusp of his professional life, God used a simple newspaper headline to get Dean's attention about his career direction. In what small ways is God speaking to you about your life?

2. Dean was deeply encouraged by Ephesians 2:10 during one of his career transitions. How does this verse speak to you? Do you find it comforting or confusing?

3. In choosing between two very good job options, Dean noted, "I don't want to miss God's best." Why should that be important? What will it take to have God's best?

• • • •

Lydia Hoyle: Guided by Peace

• • • •

1. What do you think of Lydia Hoyle's observation, "God cares more about who I am than what I do; if I'm trying to be the person God wants me to be, it will become more obvious what he wants me to do."

2. Lydia described a constant communion with God that helps her determine the direction her life

should go. What would it take for you to have that kind of connection with the Lord?

3. Seeking God's direction can lead to rough spots. Lydia noted, "Don't stop pursuing your calling when things look bad. Don't make big decisions when you can't hear beyond the rattling in your brain." What will it take to hang in there with God through the hard parts of following him?

• • • •

Jeff Gordon: Who Owns My Soul?

• • • •

1. Jeff Gordon describes a major challenge to his career philosophy when fellow doctors said another physician had "sold his soul" to the corporation. What do you think about the way he handled that? Would you have handled it any differently?

2. Doctors typically spend four years in some kind of pre-med training, four years in med school, and three to five years in residency. They could spend extra time in residency for a specialty. What do you think of Jeff's decision to use his medical training in more of a secondary way, as a means to support his service in the church?

3. Jeff said, "Each step of scaling back, it's been God saying, 'Here's an opportunity, which way do you want to go?' It's not like I said, 'I don't like this so I'm going to dump it and find something else to do.' I get suspicious of that kind of thinking." What do you think about that? What point is Jeff making?

· · · ·

Section 3: Potential Outcomes
Home Life

· · · ·

1. How would changing your life affect things at home? What adjustments would you need to make? How about your spouse?

2. Dave Howard admits that his approach to Christian work left a gap at home. How could Dave have changed that situation while still pursuing the Lord?

3. What would it take for you to have a Great Commission family—a family working together to reach out to non-Christians and help Christians grow? How would your priorities and schedule have to change?

4. How do you think God may want to transform you as a spouse? As a parent?

· · · ·

Ministry

· · · ·

1. What do you think when you hear the word *ministry*? How does the biblical description, based on Galatians 6 and other passages, match your view?

2. Write down your areas of expertise, your talents, and your spiritual gifts. Consider doing this: put the list on your own personal altar—the mantle, the

dresser—and offer them to God as a gift; ask him to show you how to use them for His purposes.

3. Are you part of a home based Bible study? What does that group look like? Do you feel you have an important role there? Does your small group have a Great Commission mission? Why or why not?

4. With whom in your life could you begin a discipleship relationship? If you don't know, pray about it for a couple weeks.

• • • •

Yourself

• • • •

1. Roll back the years for a minute. What kind of a ten-year-old were you? What predictions did people make about you then? What kind of a person have you turned out to be? How did you get there?

2. As you look at how God may want to change you, what areas concern you the most?

3. I discuss three areas where I've experienced transformation: in my emotional life, my creativity, and developing an unguarded attitude. What kind of changes might God do in you? What kind of changes would you like to see?

4. What do you think of the changes in Saul/Paul? Do you think they were positive? Why or why not?

• • • •

Section 4: Grasping the Big Picture
It's About Your Whole Life

• • • •

1. Respond to this statement: The safest place in the world is right next to Jesus. Do you believe that? Why or why not?

2. Where do you go for security when something rocks your world? What do you think about to steady yourself and give yourself a sense of stability?

3. There are many areas of life we should present to the Lord. What area do you hesitate to give to God? Why?

• • • •

It's About Your Relationship with God

• • • •

1. How much time do you spend reading the Bible in a week; a month; a year? What goal could you set for yourself to increase your time in the Word?

2. I talk about "truth snacking." Is that something you do? What verses do you like to munch on during a day? What verses do you ponder when you need encouragement to follow God?

3. How would you describe your prayer life?

4. Do you have Christian friends who "wound" you as described in Proverbs 27:6? Why or why not? If not, start praying today for another Christian per-

son who wants to seek Christ and grow with you. Pray that prayer for a couple weeks.

• • • •

It's About Spiritual Warfare

• • • •

1. What do you think of my observation that when you give God your lifestyle and priorities, you're telling him you're ready for battle? Do you agree? Why would that get Satan's attention?

2. I make this statement: "Following God will get intense. You must be convinced there's life beyond this existence and God's evaluation of you in the next life matters more than the evaluation of any other person in this one." Why would this be important?

3. How do you normally evaluate negative thoughts about your identity? Have you ever thought of those as coming from the devil? Why would Satan use this approach?

4. The devil uses a variety of attacks, from negative personal thoughts to cynical comments by friends or family. Which do you fear the most? Why? How can you deal with those?

• • • •

Section 5: One Last Push
There's Hope

• • • •

1. Can you relate to the comments at the beginning of the chapter, "I'll never grow into something more than what I've become; I've messed things up too much; I'm too set in my ways; the die is cast." Why do you feel that way? Can you see the possibility of change? Where would it start?

2. Have you sensed God wooing you during the reading of this book? Great! How?

3. Are you sensing God's tugging on you to make some changes? Write down what those may be. Or brainstorm with a friend about the changes God wants you to pursue and how to get there.

Endnotes

Paul: The Leather Craftsman

1. Martin Robinson and Dwight Smith, *Invading Secular Space* (Oxford: Monarch Books, 2003), 62–63.

2. "The Barna Group." 2008. The Barna Group, Ltd. "Stewardship." <http://www.barna.org/> (January 2008).

3. Dennis McCallum, "Philippians 3: Knowing Christ" (Columbus, Ohio: Xenos Christian Fellowship, 2008).

Donna Jordan-Mitchell: A Better Epitaph

4. Launch Foundation Inc. 2006. "History." <http://www.launchfoundation.org/>

Section 3: Potential Outcomes

5. "World of Words: A Quote from George Leigh Mallory." <http://www.AskOxford.com/>. Oxford Dictionaries. 2008.

Home Life

6. "EurekAlert." American Association for the Advancement of Science, "Ohio working family survey shows women still do most housework." (Cincinnati: University of Cincinnati, 1998).

Yourself

7. American Art Therapy Association Inc. 2008.

8. ardent gardens, llc. "Gardens." <http://www.ardent-gardens.com/>

9. *Merriam-Webster Online Dictionary.* 2008. "Goad." <http://www.merriam-webster.com/>

10. Keener, Craig S. *The IVP Bible Background Commentary: New Testament.* Downers Grove, IL: InterVarsity Press, 1993, 399.

It's About Your Whole Life

11. *Funk & Wagnalls Standard Encyclopedic Dictionary.* "Quotations: Nature." Chicago: J.G. Ferguson Publishing Co., 1975. 950.

12. Wayne Watson, *The Way Home*, Nashville: Word Records, 1998.

There's Hope

13. Crabb, Larry, *Shattered Dreams: God's Unexpected Pathway to Joy.* (Colorado Springs, CO:WaterBrook Press, 2001), 166.

Bibliography

American Art Therapy Association Inc. 2008. <http://www.arttherapy.org/>

Ardent Gardens, LLC. <http://www.ardentgardens.org/>

"World of Words: A Quote from George Leigh Mallory." <http://www.AskOxford.com/> Oxford Dictionaries. 2008.

The Barna Group. 2008. The Barna Group, Ltd. "Stewardship." <http://www.barna.org/> (January 2008).

"EurekAlert." American Association for the Advancement of Science. 2008. "Ohio working family survey shows women still do most housework." Cincinnati: University of Cincinnati, 1998. 30 October 2004. <http://www.eurekalert.org/>

Keener, Craig S. *The IVP Bible Background Commentary: New Testament.* Downers Grove: InterVarsity Press, 1993.

Launch Foundation Inc. 2006. <http://www. launchfoundation.org/>

Robinson, Martin and Dwight Smith. *Invading Secular Space.* Oxford: Monarch Books, 2003.

Watson, Wayne. *The Way Home.* Nashville: Word Records, 1998.

McCallum, Dennis. "Philippians 3: Knowing Christ." Columbus, Ohio: Xenos Christian Fellowship, 2008. <http://www.xenos.org/>

About the Author

Clem Boyd has worked as an advertising copywriter, healthcare public relations person, and newspaper reporter and editor. In 1992 he faced a dilemma—continue a career in newspaper journalism or change courses toward a master's degree in biblical studies. He chose the latter, but walking through that process and facing other important decisions since has caused him to reflect on what it means to follow God.

Clem has served as pastor and elder for his church, Xenos Christian Fellowship of Dayton, and has his own freelance writing business. His articles have appeared in *Focus on the Family* magazine and many of its sister publications, as well as in *Christianity Today, Christian Parenting Today, Plain Truth, Sports Spectrum,* and others. Many can be found through his web-site, www.clemboyd.com.

Clem graduated with a bachelor's degree in journalism from Ohio University in 1984 and a master's degree in biblical studies from Cincinnati Bible Seminary in 1995. He and wife Julia have three children: David, Bethany, and Mark. They have a dog, Chinook; two cats, Odie and Adda; and a bird, Sparky. Clem's mom, Jean, lives with them to complete the family.